Guitar Clinic

by

Bruce Arnold

Muse Eek Publishing Company
New York, New York

Copyright © 2001 by Muse Eek Publishing Company. All rights reserved

ISBN 1-890944-86-6

No part of this publication may be reproduced, stored in a
retrieval system, or transmitted, in any form or by any means,
electronic, mechanical, photocopying, recording, or otherwise,
without the prior written permission of the publisher.

Printed in the United States

This publication can be purchased from your local bookstore or by contacting:
Muse Eek Publishing Company
P.O. Box 509
New York, NY 10276, USA
Phone: 212-473-7030
Fax: 212-473-4601
http://www.muse-eek.com
sales@muse-eek.com

Table Of Contents

Acknowledgements	*iii*
About the Author	*iv*
Foreword	*v*
Introduction	1
Understanding Rhythm	2
Counting Rhythm	6
Performance Directions	7
Straight Eighth vs. Swing	8
Reading Example 22	9
Reading Example 23	10
Reading Example 24	11
Performance Directions	12
Performance Directions	13
Reading Example 25	14
Reading Example 26	15
Reading Example 25	16
Reading Example 26	17
Sight Reading	18
Beat Reading	20
Music Theory	21
Music Theory and Chord Construction	22
Basic Intervals Worksheet	36
Major Triads Worksheet	37
Chord Tones and Tensions Dominant 7th	38
Dominant 7#11 b13 Worksheet	39
Answers for Worksheets	40
Basic Intervals Answers	41
Major Triads Answers	42
Dominant 7#11 b13 Answers	43
Scales	44
Major Scale	45
Dorian Scale	46
Major Scale Exercises	47
Dorian Scale Exercises	51
Major Scale Answers	55
Dorian Scale Answers	59
Blank Worksheet	63
Fingering for Scales	64
Major Scale Fingering	65
Dorian Scale Fingering	66
Pentatonic Scales	67
Major Pentatonic Scale Fingering	68
Minor Pentatonic Scale Fingering	69
Blues Scales	70
Blues Scale Fingering	71
Chords	72
Moveable Chord Forms	73
Chord Voicings for Progression	74
Minor Blues Progression	77
Upper four string voicings	78
Chord Voicings for Progression	80
Blues Progression	82
Bass and Chords Comping	83
Bass and Chords Progression	85
Improvisation/Reharmonization	86
Modal Sequencing	87
Approach Notes	93
12 Chromatic Approach Notes Figures	94
12 Diatonic Approach Notes Figures	95
Technical Exercise for Approach Notes	96
Approach Note Usage	97
Chord Reharmonization	98
Hexatonics	100
Technical Exercise for Hexatonics	101
Other Tertial Hexatonics	102
Technical Exercise for Hexatonics	103
Non Tertial Hexatonics	104
Technical Exercise for Hexatonics	105
Hexatonics in Composition/Improv	106
Further Applications of Hexatonics	106
Integer Notation	107

Acknowledgements

The author would like to thank Michal Shapiro for proof reading and suggestions, and also the many students who, through their questions at clinics helped me to understand the kind of information they most needed.

About the Author

Bruce Arnold is from Sioux Falls, South Dakota. His educational background started with 3 years of music study at the University of South Dakota; he then attended the Berklee College of Music where he received a Bachelor of Music degree in composition. During that time he also studied privately with Jerry Bergonzi and Charlie Banacos.

Mr. Arnold has taught at some of the most prestigious music schools in America, including the New England Conservatory of Music, Dartmouth College, Berklee College of Music, Princeton University and New York University. He is a performer, composer, jazz clinician and has an extensive private instruction practice.

Currently Mr. Arnold is performing with his own "The Bruce Arnold Trio," and "Eye Contact" with Harvie Swartz, as well as with two experimental bands, "Release the Hounds" a free improv group, and "Spooky Actions" which re-interprets the work of 20th Century classical masters.

His debut CD "Blue Eleven" (MMC 2036J) received great critical acclaim, and his most recent CD "A Few Dozen" was released in January 2000. The Los Angeles Times said of this release "Mr. Arnold deserves credit for his effort to expand the jazz palette."

For more information about Mr. Arnold check his website at http://www.arnoldjazz.com This website contains audio examples of Mr. Arnold's compositions and a workshop section with free downloadable music exercises.

Foreword

I wrote this book to address the common questions asked, and common problems I find among students who attend the many clinics I give each year. The guitar student is, in a way, a special type of student. Many are self taught, and have no formal training. They have learned either through listening, word of mouth, or from books or magazines. Consequently there are frequent misunderstandings of simple to advanced concepts along with general misconceptions about what kind of discipline it takes to be a great guitarist.

Guitar is one of the hardest instruments to master. From its asymmetrically tuned strings, to its many repeated notes it is a real challenge for a player of any level to organize and develop even the simplest musical concepts.

This book presents a general overview of the major courses of study a serious guitar student should follow. It's just the tip of the iceberg, so as each musical concept is presented, further study recommendations are given for the student who wishes to become a master musician.

Muse Eek Publishing has created a website with a FAQ forum for all my books. If you have any questions about anything contained in this book feel free to contact me at FAQ@muse-eek.com and I will happy to post an answer to your question. My goal is to educate and help you reach a higher degree of musical ability.

Bruce Arnold
New York, New York

Introduction

Welcome to the Guitar Clinic!

This book will give you helpful information to clarify and expand on the techniques presented at the clinics I teach. Because of the wide variations of ability in students who attend these clinics, you will find exercises and examples here that range greatly in difficulty. If you have a desire to become an excellent musician (which I'm figuring is the reason you are at this clinic or have bought this book) you need to make sure that you understand and are proficient in all the material presented. Students of any level should make sure that they are not neglecting important abilities like being able to read music, understanding music theory and knowing the names of the notes and where they occur on the guitar.

This book is not meant to be a complete course on mastering the guitar; you should work on the exercises presented and if you have problems with a particular exercise you should look into purchasing the book that the exercise comes from, so that you can work more fully on correcting your weaknesses.

If at anytime you have further questions about your next step or any specific question you can always e-mail me at faq@muse-eek.com and your question will be posted on the muse-eek.com website, along with an answer. As an owner of this book you are also entitled to enter the "members section" of the muse-eek website where there is further educational information in the form of text, videos and audio to help you in the learning process. (See the muse-eek.com website for details.) Note that most of the musical examples in this book can be found in the form of midifiles on the muse-eek.com website.

This book covers the major weaknesses and misconceptions commonly found among guitarists. It will cover the following subjects:

1. Reading
2. Rhythm
3. Music Theory: both chord construction and scale construction
4. Scale positions on the guitar fretboard
5. Chord voicings: both root positions and inversions
6. Walking bass and chords
7. Improvisation Techniques, including Scales (Modal Sequencing), Approach Note Theory, Chord Reharmonization and Hexatonics.

The improvisation section presents two common improvisational methods and one more advanced type. Of course there are many more improvisational methods available.

Although I present it in detail at all clinics I give, to keep this book affordable I have not included a discussion of ear training with the necessary accompanying CDs. Ear training requires a two part approach of listening and singing exercises. I recommend you look into the following books to develop your ear training skills.

1. Ear Training: One Note Beginning   ISBN #1890944122
2. Ear Training: One Note Intermediate   ISBN #1890944130
3. Ear Training: One Note Advanced   ISBN #1890944149
4. Fanatic's Guide to Sight Singing and Ear Training   ISBN #189094419X

Please see the muse-eek website for help on what level is best for your current ability. I can't stress enough that developing your ear is of paramount importance to becoming a great musician.

So let's get started. First we need to discuss rhythm. If you already understand how to read rhythm and how music is represented on a staff you can move on to page 7-8 for directions and begin reading the rhythm exercises on page 9.

For those of you who have no experience reading music the following pages give an explanation of how rhythm is presented in written form. If you don't understand what the notes are on a music staff, please see page 22 for help with reading notes on the guitar.

Understanding Rhythm

The rhythm in a piece of music is presented in overall units call "measures" These measures are further divided up into beats. (more on this in a moment) Example One shows you one "measure" of music. There are many different symbols in a measure of music. These symbols show how to play the music. To the far left there is always a clef sign. This tells the reader what pitch level the notes will be on the staff. The clef sign used here is the treble clef sign, therefore the 4 notes presented in this measure would be four middle C's. (for more explanation, go to page 22). The next symbol is the time signature. This tells you how the measure will be divided rhythmically. In this case the time signature is 4/4. The top 4 tells you how many beats are in a measure. In this case the measure has 4 beats in it. The bottom 4 tells you what unit of measure will be used to show those 4 beats. In this case the 4 represents a quarter note. So this whole measure is divided up into 4 quarters and these 4 quarters are each represented by a note called a quarter note. A quarter note would be held for one beat. A line is placed at the end of each measure to show where the end of each measure is. Audio files for the examples presented here can be found on the muse-eek.com website.

Example 1

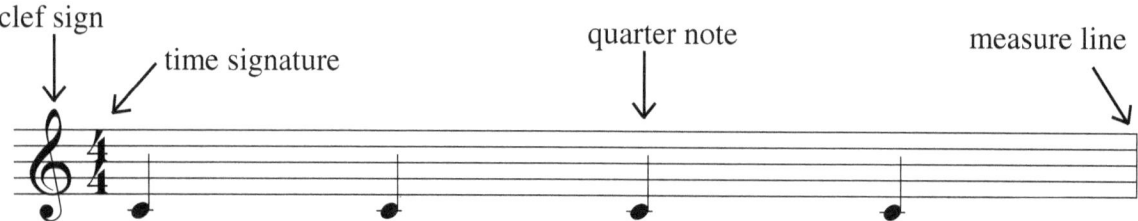

Rhythm can of course be much more or less complicated than example 1. In example 2 we still have a 4/4 measure and it still has only 4 beats in the measure but we have only one note which happens on beat one. This note takes up all four beats of the measure so you would sustain the sound for four beats. This note is called a whole note. Example 3 shows a measure that has been divided up into two equal parts. These notes are called half notes and because we have a 4/4 measure there can only be 2 half notes in a measure because a half note gets 2 beats. The first note is played on beat one and the second note is played on beat 3.

Example 2

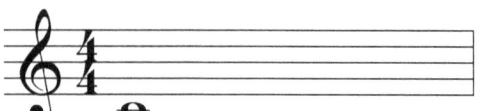

Example 3

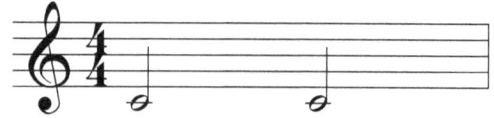

As I have said, rhythm can be much more complicated than the previous example. In example 4 we still have a 4/4 measure and it still has only 4 beats in the measure but each beat has been divided into equal divisions to form a new rhythm. So now rather than just four rhythmic hits in the measure there are eight. These new notes are referred to as eighth notes because it takes 8 eighth notes to make up one measure of 4/4. So for each beat you would play two notes equally dividing that beat into two parts.

Example 4

Rhythm can be further subdivided. In example 5 each beat has been subdivided into three equal parts. These three note groups are commonly called triplets and usually have a bracket and a number three placed above the grouping. Therefore you would play three notes for each beat equally dividing that beat into three parts.

Example 5

We can also divide each beat into 4 equal parts. In example 6 each beat has been subdivided into four equal parts. Each note of this four note grouping is called a sixteenth note. Therefore you would play four notes for each beat, equally dividing that beat into four parts.

Example 6

We can also divide each beat into eight equal parts. In example 7 each beat has been subdivided into 8 equal parts. Each note of this eight note grouping is called a thirty second note. Therefore you would play eight notes for each beat equally dividing that beat into eight parts.

Example 7

Rests

Each of the rhythms presented in the previous 7 examples could leave some notes out to create other rhythms. These left out notes are called rests and use the symbols shown below. During the rests you don't play anything. You will see in the forthcoming examples that when rests are placed into measures the rhythm can become quite complex. We will start with some simple examples.

Examples 8-10 show measures with three kinds of rests. In example 8 there is a whole note rest. Nothing would be played during this measure. Example 9 shows a half note rest. In this case nothing would be played for the first two beats of the measure. Example 10 shows a quarter note rest. In this case nothing would be played for beat 3 of this measure.

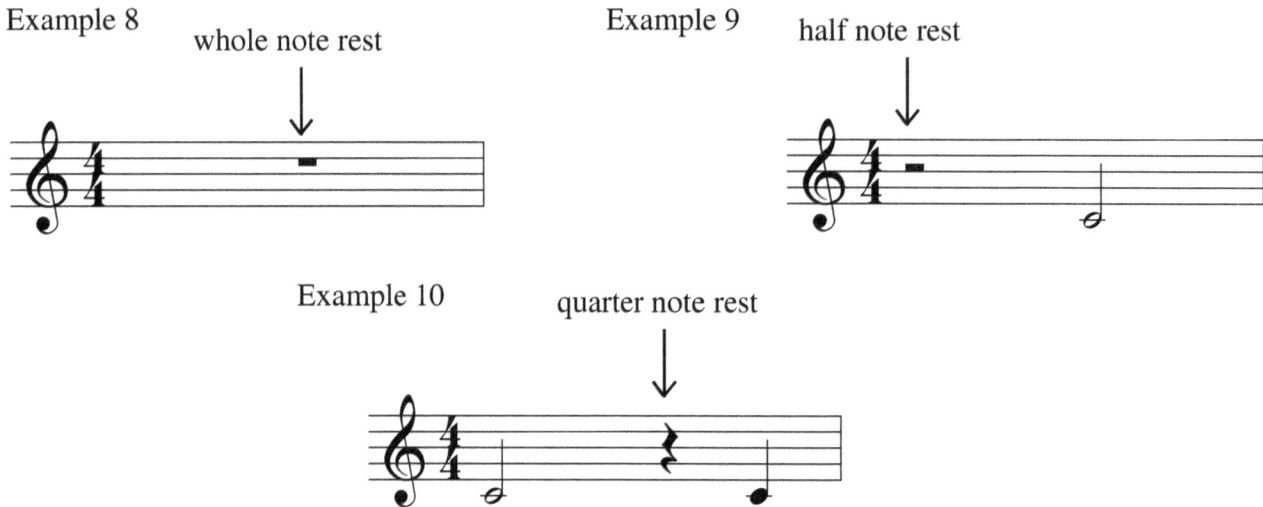

Examples 11-12 show measures that are composed of eighth notes but in which some of the eighth notes have been left out.

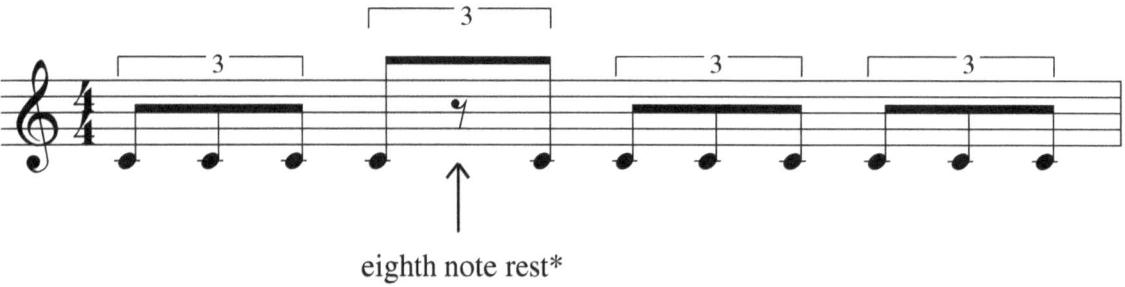

*Note: Eighth notes within a triplet receive 1/3 of a beat. Therefore when an eighth note rest is found within a triplet the eighth note rest equals 1/3 of a beat.

Example 13 shows you a sixteenth note rhythm where a sixteenth note rest has been added.

Example 13

sixteenth note rest

Example 14 shows you a thirty second note rhythm where a thirty second note rest has been added.

Example 14

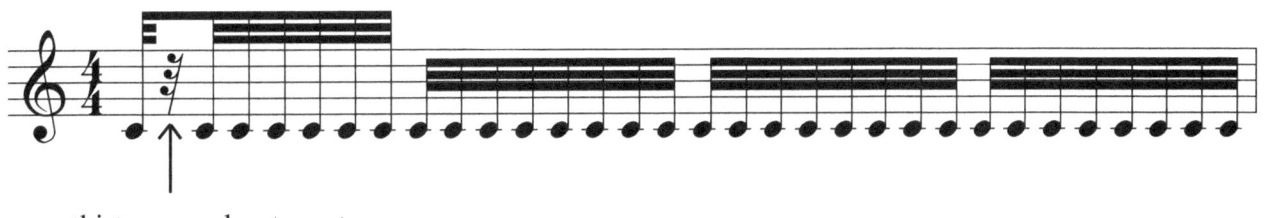

thirty second note rest

A measure can contain a variety of rests. Example 15 shows you a measure with various types of rests.

Example 15

* A sixteenth note is written with two *flags* on its right side to indicate its value when found alone.

Dots

A dot can be placed after a note or rest to lengthen its value. A dot adds 1/2 of the note's value, therefore in example 16, the dot placed after the eighth note rest adds a one sixteenth rest, totalling a rest of three sixteenths. (One eighth plus one sixteenth = 3 sixteenths.) Example 17 shows the same situation but with a note rather than a rest.

Example 16   dot   Example 17

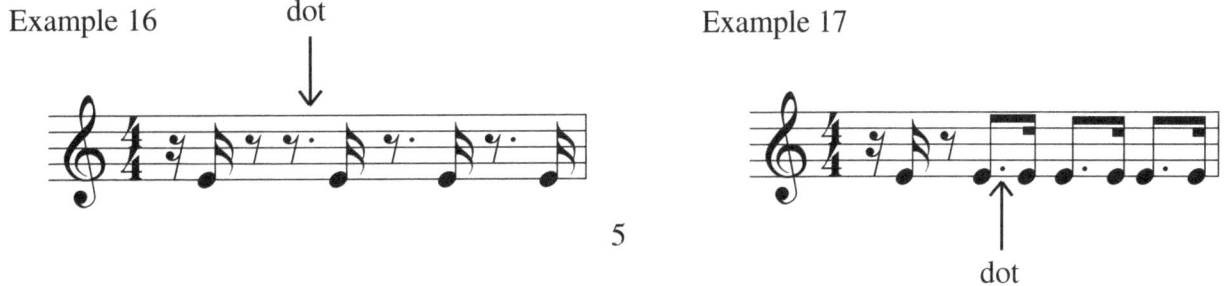

dot

Ties

Ties can also be placed into music to lengthen a particular note. Example 18 shows two quarter notes tied together. Example 19 shows what this rhythm would sound like.

Example 18

Example 19

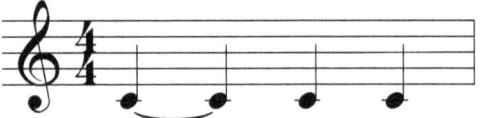

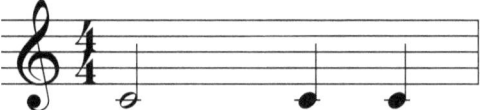

Counting

Although I don't recommend it as a long term habit, a beginner often needs a method to help count each beat and subdivision. Over time you should develop the ability to recognize any rhythm and know what it sounds like. But again, if you are a beginner or you are having a problem with a rhythm, counting is a way to work it through. The follow examples give the counting method I recommend.

1 2 3 4

1 and 2 and 3 and 4 and

Tri pu let Tri pu let Tri pu let Tri pu let
or 1 2 3 1 2 3 1 2 3 1 2 3

1 e and ah 2 e and ah 3 e and ah 4 e and ah
or 1 2 3 4 1 2 3 4 1 2 3 4 1 2 3 4

1 2 3 4 5 6 7 8 1 2 3 4 5 6 7 8 1 2 3 4 5 6 7 8 1 2 3 4 5 6 7 8

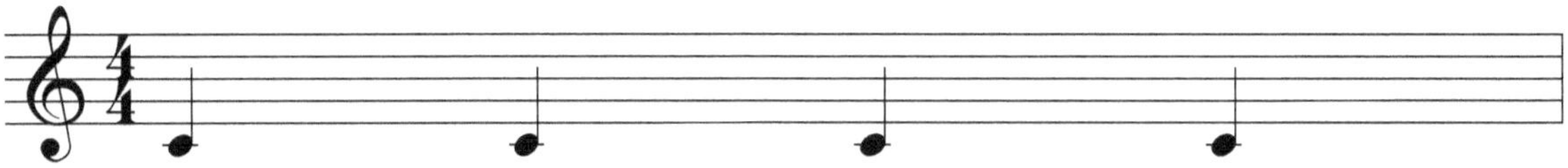

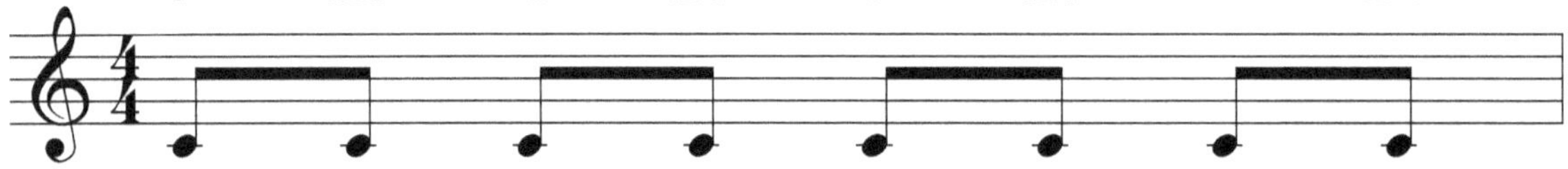

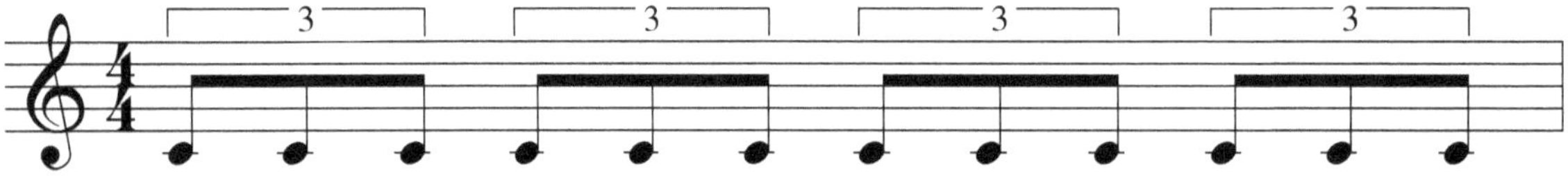

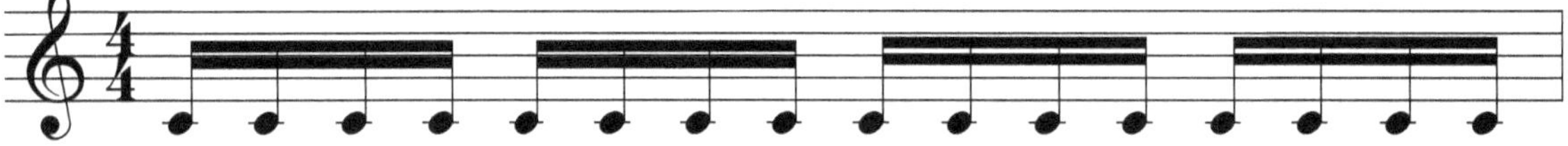

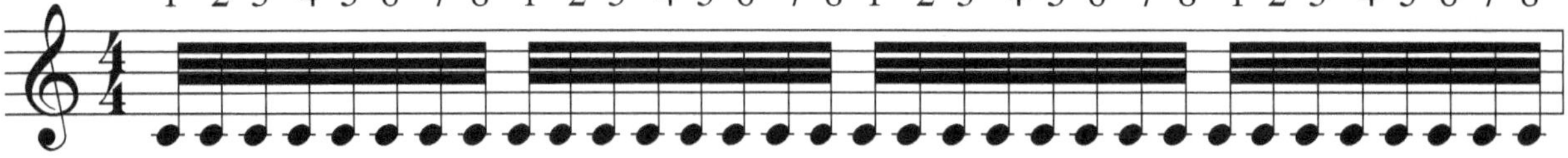

Rhythm Exercises

On pages 9-11 you will find three rhythm exercises. These exercises employ no rests and limited ties. The difficulty of these exercises all depends on the tempo. I will offer students three levels of difficulty in performing these exercises. Please see below for directions for each level.

Metric Levels

Different styles of music use different metric levels of music notation. These different metric levels make it easier for a musician to read music written for particular styles. The example found on page 9 shows a metric level which contains mostly whole, half and quarter notes. This metric level is commonly used in music that is played at a fast tempo. Therefore it is common to find this notation with fast jazz charts and other music which is played at a fast tempo.

Page 10 is written in a metric level that contains mostly quarter and eighth notes. This metric level is commonly used for medium tempo jazz, rock and is the most common metric level used.

Page 11 is written in a metric level that contains mostly eighths and sixteenths. This metric level is commonly found in funk and some slower rock tunes.

Performance Directions

There are midifiles on the muse-eek.com website to help you with these exercises

Page 9-Example 23

Beginning Level:

Play page 9 at a slow tempo. Start at metronome = 60 for a quarter note. Work your way up to quarter note = 120.

Intermediate Level:

Play page 9 at half note = 60. The metronome should click on beats one and three. Work your way up to half note = 120.

Advanced Level:

Play page 9 at whole note = 60. The metronome should click only on beat one. Work your way up to whole note = 120.

If you would like more examples of this type of rhythmic exercise please see the book "Rhythm Primer" ISBN#1890944033

Page 10-Example 24

Beginner Level:

Play page 10 at a slow tempo. Start at metronome = 60 for a quarter note. Work your way up to quarter note = 120.

Intermediate Level:

Play page 10 at half note = 60. The metronome should click on beats one and three. Work your way up to half note = 120. Also try having the metronome click on beats two and four. Play both as a straight eighth feel and a swing feel. See page 8 for explanation of eighth vs. swing feels.

Advanced Level:

Play page 10 at whole note = 60. The metronome should click only on beat one. Work your way up to whole note = 120. Play both as a straight eighth feel and a swing feel . See page 8 for explanation of eighth vs. swing feels.

If you would like more examples of this type of rhythmic exercise please see the book "Rhythm Primer" ISBN#1890944033

Page 11-Example 24

Beginner Level:
Play page 11 at a slow tempo. Start at metronome = 60 for a quarter note. Work your way up to quarter note = 120.

Intermediate Level:
Play page 11 at half note = 60. The metronome should click on beats one and three. Work your way up to half note = 120. Also try having the metronome click on beats two and four. Play both as a straight eighth feel and a swing feel. See below for explanation of eighth vs. swing feels.

Advanced Level:
Play page 11 at whole note = 60. The metronome should click only on beat one. Work your way up to whole note = 120. Play both as a straight eighth feel and a swing feel. See below for explanation of eighth vs. swing feels.

If you would like more examples of this type of rhythmic exercise please see the book "Rhythm Primer" ISBN#1890944033

Straight Eighth vs. Swing Eighth Note Feel

Different styles of music interpret the written eighth note in different ways. Rock and Latin music in general play written music "as written," in other words you just play the notes as you see them.* On the other hand with a "swing feel" which is commonly found in jazz and blues, you play the eighth note with more of a triplet feel. If you have a measure of eighth notes as in example 20 you would play these eighth notes like a triplet but leaving out the middle note. (see example 21)

Example 20

Example 21

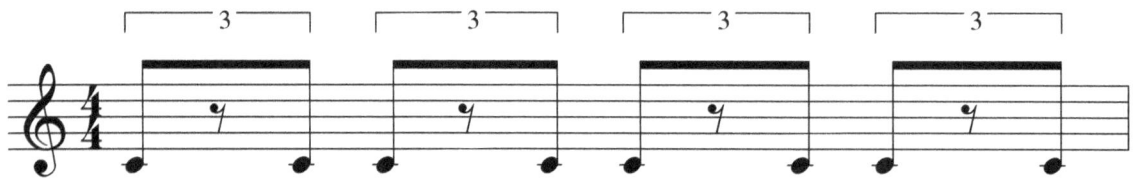

* There are slight deviations among all performers and styles as far as note interpretation goes. It should be kept in mind that examples 20 and 21 are only approximations of how eighth notes are played. Upon closer analysis you will find slight variations between any two styles of interpretation. It is recommended that you transcibe and learn melodies and solos of great jazz, rock and blues players to experience this difference first hand.

Example 22

Excerpt from "Rhythm Primer" ISBN#1890944033

Example 23
Excerpt from "Rhythm Primer" ISBN#1890944033

Example 24
Excerpt from "Rhythm Primer" ISBN#1890944033

The next three examples incorporate rests and ties into the exercise. Example 25 contains rhythms commonly found in jazz music. Example 26 contains rhythms commonly found in funk music. Example 27 contains rhythms common to ballads. Use the performance directions below to work on these exercises. The metronome markings are set to cover the typical speeds that you will find music written in with each metric level.

Performance Directions

Page 14-Example 25

Beginning Level:
    Play page 14 at a slow tempo. Start at metronome = 50 for a quarter note. Work your way up to quarter note = 100.

Intermediate Level:
    Play page 14 at half note = 60. The metronome should click on beats one and three. Work your way up to half note = 120. Also try having the metronome click on beats two and four. Play both as a straight eighth feel and a swing feel. See page 8 for explanation of eighth vs. swing feels

Advanced Level:
    Play page 14 at whole note = 40. The metronome should click only on beat one. Work your way up to whole note = 60. Play both as a straight eighth feel and a swing feel. See page 8 for explanation of eighth vs. swing feels.

If you would like more examples of this type of rhythmic exercise please see the book "Rhythms Volume One" ISBN# 0964863278

Page 15-Example 26

Beginner Level:
    Play page 15 at a slow tempo. Start at metronome = 50 for a quarter note. Work your way up to quarter note = 80.

Intermediate Level:
    Play page 15 at metronome = 60 for a quarter note. Work your way up to quarter note = 100.

Advanced Level:
    Play page 15 at metronome = 80 for a quarter note. Work your way up to quarter note = 120.

If you would like more examples of this type of rhythmic exercise please see the book "Rhythms Volume Two" ISBN# 0964863286

Page 16-Example 27

Beginner Level:

Play page 16 at a slow tempo. Start at metronome = 60 for an eighth note. Work your way up to quarter note = 80. It is not recommended that you feel time in eighth notes when playing thirty second note rhythms. Beginners may find it useful to subdivide each beat until they feel more comfortable with reading thirty second note rhythms.

Intermediate Level:

Play page 16 at quarter note = 40. Work your way up to quarter note = 50.

Advanced Level:

Play page 16 at quarter note = 50. Work your way up to quarter note = 60.

If you would like more examples of this type of rhythmic exercise please see the book "Rhythms Volume 3" ISBN# 0964863041

Odd Meters

Page seventeen has an excerpt from "Odd Meters Volume One" ISBN# 0964863294. In order to master odd meter reading you need to develop the proper way of counting through changing time signatures. If you have an eighth based meter you count in whole numbers. For instance if you have a 3/8 measure you would count (1,2,3) or a 5/8 measure would be (1,2,3,4,5). If you have a four based meter you would count (1 and 2 and) etc., so a 4/4 measure would be (1 and 2 and 3 and 4 and). A 3/4 measure would be (1 and 2 and 3 and). So if you had a 3/8 measure followed by a 2/4 measure you would count it (1,2,3) (1 and 2 and). I recommend you count out loud at first to make sure you are processing each measure correctly.

There are many recommended ways of working with this exercise. The performance directions below will give you metronome markings for just reading the page as is. There are many other applications for example 28 that I commonly recommend my students to do:

1. You can use this exercise to develop your ability as an accompanist by playing a typical progression through the exercise. I commonly have students play a I vi ii V I progression in any key making each measure a different chord.

2. Record the aforementioned I vi ii V I progression, and solo over it. This will develop your ability to solo through odd time signatures.

3. When you feel comfortable with the previously mentioned measure counting scheme you should try and tap your foot at the beginning of each measure. You could also divide larger measures up into subdivisions. For instance a 6/8 measure could be felt in 2 (i.e. tapping your foot on one and four) Or for a 9/8 measure could tap your foot on 1, 4, and 7.

Performance Directions

Page 17-Example 28

All Levels:

Play page 17 at a slow tempo. Start at metronome = 80 for a eighth note. It is recommended that you don't use a metronome for this exercise.

Example 25
Excerpt from "Rhythms Volume One" ISBN# 0964863278

Example 26

Excerpt from "Rhythms Volume Two" ISBN# 0964863286

Example 27
Excerpt from "Rhythms Volume 3" ISBN# 0964863041

Example 28
Excerpt from "Odd Meters Volume One" ISBN# 0964863294

Sight Reading

Pages 9 through 17 covered different types of rhythm on several metric levels. All these exercises are good for mastering rhythm but they are also useful for learning how to sight read. Non-classical guitarists are generally the weakest sight readers. This is caused by a lack of formal music education and the fact that the guitar is an extremely hard instrument to read on. The difficulty stems from the many different places the same note can occur on the fretboard. For example the note C found on the 1st fret of the B string can also be found on the 5th fret of the G string, the 10th fret of the D string, the 15th fret of the A string, and the 20th fret of the low E string. So if you see this note written in a piece of music it is very difficult to know where to place this note on the guitar fretboard. Also the guitar is a transposing instrument, sounding an octave below where written. In example 29 you have a middle C written. This note would be played on the 3rd fret of the A string or the 8th fret of the low E string. In reality the note that you are playing is sounding an octave below (see example 30). If you check this with a piano keyboard you will hear how your instrument is sounding an octave below where written. Also see page 35 for further explanation of the guitar as a transposing instrument.

Example 29   Example 30

To develop your sight reading skills you need to read every day. I recommend checking music out of your local library to read. The are a few basic approaches you need to develop and understand when trying to improve your reading skills. They are listed below:

    1. Read many different types of sheet music; from classical to jazz. Read music written for other instruments, read from scores and parts. Reading from as many different types of written manuscripts as possible will help your eye to feel comfortable with any kind of music you have to read. I would also recommend using the "Rhythm" series, parts of which have been excerpted in the previous pages. A complete list of these books can be found in the back of this book.

    2. Find a comfortable tempo to read each piece of music. Slow the music down to a point where you don't have to stop anywhere, but can continue through the entire piece. This is very important! Many students develop a habit of stopping when they reach a difficult passage. Then when they are sight reading in a professional situation they stop, while the band continues, and at that point they are lost. ALWAYS READ THROUGH ANY DIFFICULT PASSAGE AND KEEP YOUR PLACE IN THE MUSIC.

    3. Develop your familiarity with chord progressions and chord voicings on two levels. First you should be able to read both chord symbols and notated chord voicings. I highly recommend "Chord Workbook for Guitar" Volumes One and Two for developing this skill (see back of book for details on these books.) Secondly a guitarist is not only required to read a chord symbol as written. There are also cases where you are reading a chord chart from a fake book where you need to supply the proper type of chord based on the style of music and the movement of the overall progression.

There are many possible alterations you can make to chords to put them into a jazz style. I will give a short example of how this style/chord system works. Let me first give you a little background information. If you are a beginning student you should first read the theory section found on pages 21-35 before going any further.

Every chord has three types of notes that are associated with it.

a. The chord tones (the notes that make up its basic structure) which are usually four notes. For example in a F7b9b13 the chord tones are 1,3,5,b7

b. The available tensions. For a dominant chord the available tensions are *(b2,2,b3,#4,b6,6). The F7b9b13 in this case just uses two of those tensions. In jazz tensions are thought of as non chord tones that don't have to resolve so they can be added to chords to give them more color.

c. The final group of note(s) is/are the avoid note(s). For a dominant chord the 4th is the avoid note. An avoid note is a non-chord tone that needs to resolve. This note can be played melodically but usually isn't stressed or used to end a phrase. Avoid notes are never used in chords.

Armed with that information, let's say you come across a chord progression in a fake book that is C-7 to F7 to Bb. If you are playing in a jazz style you would add tensions to some of these chords to make them sound more stylistically correct. Let's look at each chord:

a. C-7 (C minor 7th). In general if you are playing in a jazz style a -7 doesn't have to have added tensions. On occasion tensions are added when you have a -7 that is at a very slow tempo or is played for more than one measure. In this case, however we will leave the C-7 as is because it doesn't need added tensions.

b. F7 (F dominant 7th). A dominant chord must always have added tensions. Therefore the F7 chord must be changed. I suggest adding either a tension 9 to make the chord an F9 or a tension 13 to make the chord an F13.

c. Bb (Bb major). A major chord must at least have a major 7th added, so the Bb major chord should be changed to a BbΔ7 (the symbol Δ means to add a major 7th to the chord.)

Our final progression would therefore be C-7 F9 BbΔ7 or C-7 F13 BbΔ7

There are of course many other possible tensions you could add to these chords. You can also see page 38 for more information. I recommend working through the "Chord Workbook for Guitar Volumes" One and Two for a better understanding of each chord and its available tensions. These books will also give you many chord progressions to help you learn where and when to use tensions. The "Music Theory Workbook for Guitar" Volumes One and Two will also help you to hone your theoretical skills so you can quickly process what the chord tone, tensions and avoid notes are for any chord.

*these notes are sometimes thought of as their higher extensions i.e. b9,9,#9,#11,b13,13

4. The last technique for improving your sight reading ability is the following exercise, which you will find very beneficial. This exercise called "Beat Reading" makes your eye move ahead of the music, and it utilizes a technique borrowed from speed reading courses. The basic idea is that if you can get your eye processing music in larger chunks and seeing groups of beats in larger units you will be able to read more accurately and at a faster rate. This exercise should be practiced every day. Most students find that within a week or two they notice dramatic improvement in their sight reading ability.

Beat Reading

1. Read only the note on beat one of each measure.
   If you have a tie from previous measure or a rest don't play anything

2. Read only the note on beat one and three of each measure.
   If you have a tie from previous note, measure or a rest don't play anything

3. Read only the note on every beat
   If you have a tie from previous note, measure or a rest don't play anything

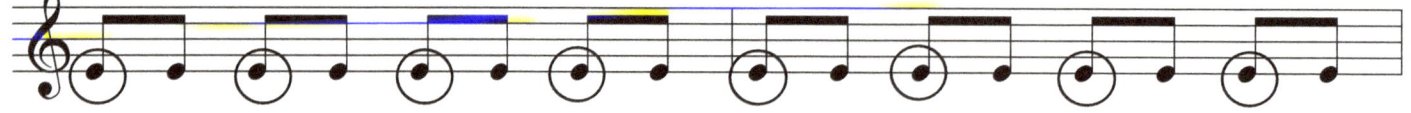

Music Theory

This music theory section (pages 21 to 43) is excerpted from the book "Music Theory Workbook for Guitar Volume One" and is highly recommended for guitarists who want to sharpen their music theory skills and get a better working knowledge on the guitar fretboard.

The Theory Workbook contains very targeted exercises. Each exercise presents a group of intervals or chords which must be written using staff notation and guitar chord diagrams. This method will instill the information in your head and your hands. Direct physical application of music theory makes it more relevant and greatly helps in learning the guitar fretboard.

Background theory information needed to complete each exercise is presented in this Clinic Book in easy to understand language. This is followed by three exercises for learning intervals, triads, and one type of 7th chord (4 note chords.) The answers to these exercises can be found on pages 41-43.

The exercises are designed for a 24 fret guitar so keep this in mind when completing the chord diagrams. The notes contained in each chord will fit into the chord diagram supplied with each exercise. Make sure to fit your answer into this diagram. You can place more than one note on each string. The answers are not meant to be played as a chord but as an arpeggio (one note after another).

For each exercise you will need to find the intervals or chord tones/tensions. Each example will require you to figure out where the notes would be on a staff and where these notes would be located on a guitar. Remember that memorizing the notes contained in each chord presented combined with knowing where these notes are on the guitar will open up a whole new understanding and command of music. Here's how each example will appear:

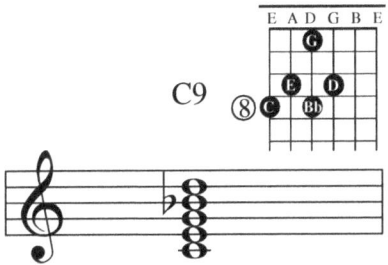

A full explanation of the chord diagrams can be found on page 34.

There are many times more than one correct answer for the worksheets presented on page 36, 37 and 39. The alternative answers to these exercise can be found in the "Members Section" of the muse-eek.com website.

Study the theory section that follows. If you wish to work on the pertinent exercises, you will find the pages on which these exercises appear given along with the theory presented. Try applying each completed exercise to songs or chord vamps you know, so that your ear can get comfortable with each new sound.

Music theory and chord construction

The first thing a student must tackle is learning how to read music. A detailed description of the development of music notation is beyond the scope of this book and some inconsistencies (which will appear in italics) have stayed in musical notation, in the course of that development. For the beginner these inconsistencies can be very confusing but inconsistent as it may be, music notation does have a standard for expressing itself visually and by understanding this system the world of western music is open to you.

In this system a series of lines and spaces are employed to create a visual representation of sound. Each line and space corresponds to a pitch. Each pitch is given a name A, B, C, D, E, F, or G. A clef sign is also used to designate what names each line and space will receive. The reason for the many types of clefs will be explained momentarily. First let us look at the treble clef. The treble clef places the note sequence in the order listed below. This complete system of lines and spaces with a clef sign is called a staff.

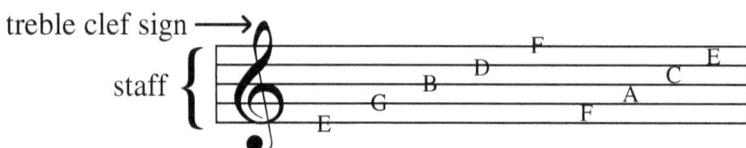

As can be seen in the examples each line and space corresponds to a different tone. If you want to have pitches higher or lower than the 5 lines and four spaces you can extend the staff by using ledger lines. Ledger lines give you the ability to represent higher and lower pitches by extending the staff, these extended pitches are called ledger line notes.

If we extend this idea we run into trouble as can be seen from the example below. When excessive ledger lines are used, reading music becomes very difficult. To alleviate this problem other clefs are employed to make reading these notes that are out of the treble clef's range easier. The note in the previous example would be found in the bass or F clef on the 2nd space.

The following example shows where the notes fall in the bass clef. We will only use the treble clef in this book but a basic understanding of the bass clef is important.

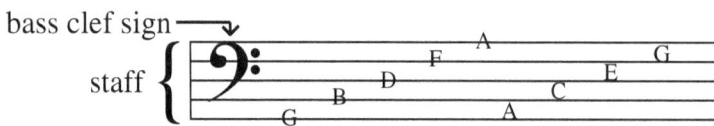

If we look at our treble clef again we notice that there is an "e" on the first line and a "e" on the 4th space. Our ear recognizes these pitches as being the same pitch but the "e" on the 4th space sounds like a higher version of the low "e". In musical terminology the higher "e" is said to sound an octave higher than the lower "e". If we play these two "e's" on the guitar it would be the 2nd fret on the D string and fifth fret on the B string.

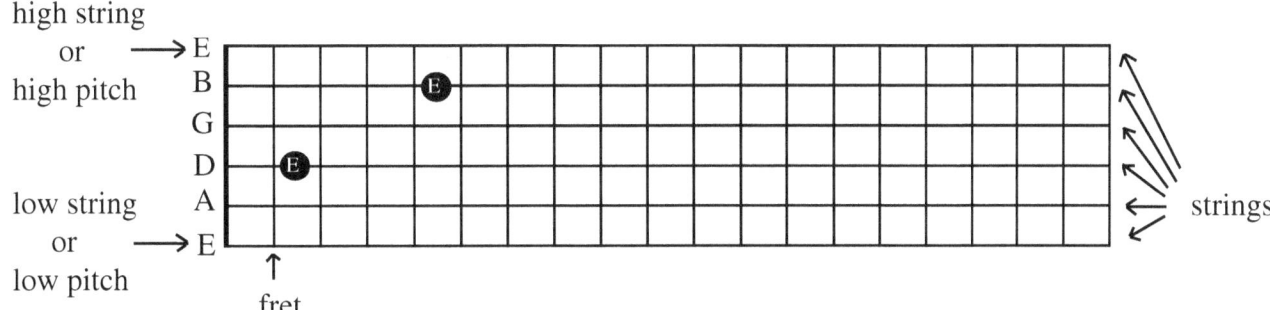

To summarize what we have learned so far: there are 7 pitches which are represented on a staff with the letter names A,B,C,D,E,F,G. These 7 pitches keep repeating themselves in different octaves. To represent these notes in other octaves we need to use ledger lines or other clefs.

One of the inconsistencies of the notation system we have learned so far is that it doesn't show all the available notes in western music. There are a total of 12 pitches used in western music which of course as we have learned can be found in many different octaves. To show all 12 notes in the system, "sharp"(#) and "flat" (b) symbols are used to represent the tones that occur between the letter names of the notes. For example between the note C and D there exists a pitch which can be called either C sharp or D flat. These notes are represented as follows: C# or Db. The (#) and (b) symbols work in the following way, the flat (b) lowers a pitch and a sharp (#) which raises the pitch. If a note is sharped it is said to have been raised a half step; if it is flatted it is said to have been lowered a half step. **A half step is the smallest distance possible in western music.** If we show all 12 notes on the staff within one octave we get what is called the chromatic scale. This scale contains all possible notes in the western system of music. Notice that there is no sharp or flat between E and F and B and C which is just one of those inconsistencies you have to accept with this notational system. Both chromatic scales shown below sound the same on the guitar; the decision to use sharps or flats depends on the musical situation. You will notice that the D in the chromatic scale with flats has a symbol in front of it. This symbol is called a natural sign. It is used to cancel the flat that appears before the previous D. **In written music, measures are used to delineate time, and sharps and flats carry through the whole measure until a new measure starts, unless a natural symbol is used to cancel it.**

Chromatic Scale

The 12 note chromatic scale can be represented by either of the two previous examples. Remember a C# is the same note as a Db on the guitar. If you play on only one string of the guitar and move consecutively up each fret you will be playing a chromatic scale. If you were to play the two previous examples of a chromatic scale you would start on the A string 3rd fret and move up each fret until you reach the 15th fret to complete the chromatic scale.

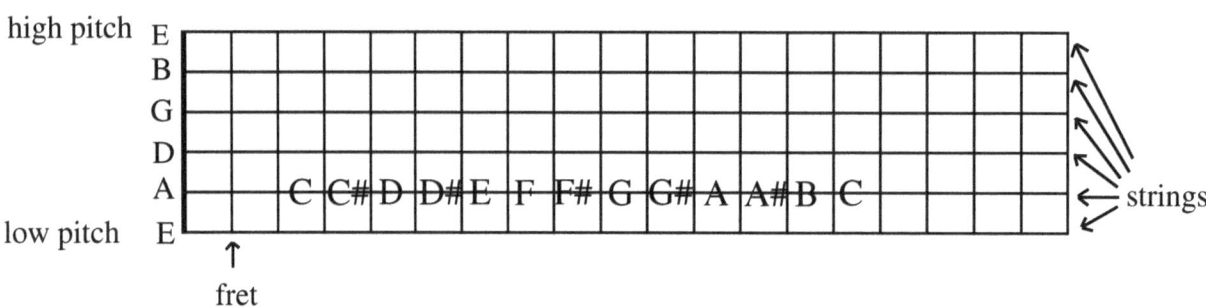

Though the chromatic scale represents all 12 notes, much of western music of the last few centuries has been based around only 7 tones. If we extract these 7 notes as shown below we end up with a major scale.

If we look at the distance in half steps between the notes of a major scale we see a pattern; whole, whole, half, whole, whole, whole, half. **All major scales are based on these intervals.**

If we apply this to the guitar fretboard the information works out accordingly: start on any note on the guitar and move up on one string starting with a whole step (2 frets), whole step, half step (1 fret), whole step, whole step, whole step, half step. This is one way to play a major scale on the guitar.

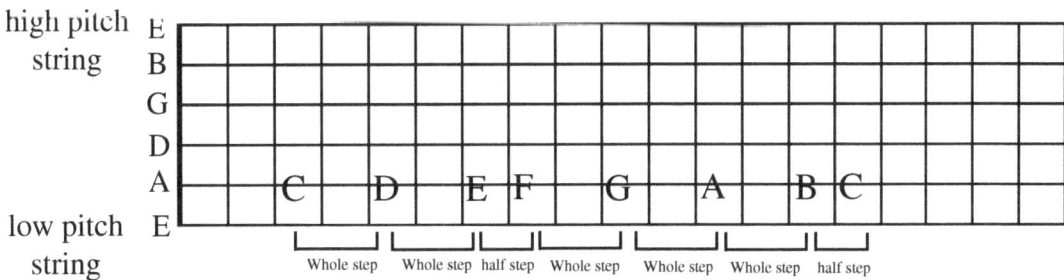

With this information you could play any major scale by following the pattern of whole step, whole step, half step, whole step, whole step, whole step, half step. The example below shows a D major scale.

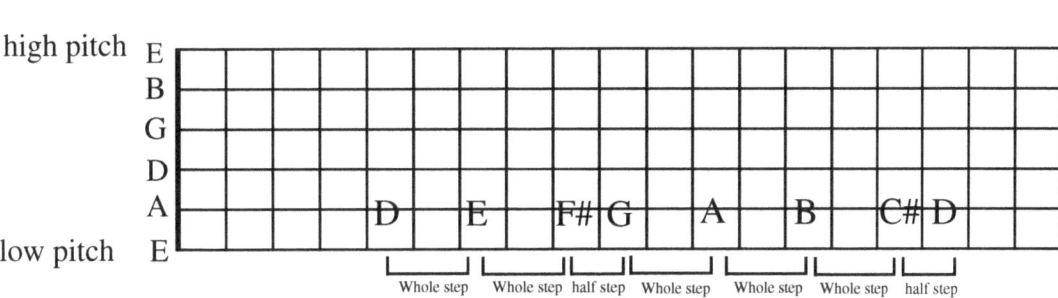

The notes of a C major scale C, D, E, F, G, A, B are commonly referred to as the diatonic notes of the key of C major. If we had the key of D major the diatonic notes would be D, E, F#, G, A, B, C#

If we use the major scale formula (1,1,1/2,1,1,1,1/2) we can figure out every major scale. We will find that each key has a different number of sharps or flats. If a piece of music uses a particular key, its key signature is placed at the beginning of the piece of music. The following is a list of all the sharps and flats found in various keys. These are commonly referred to as the key signatures, and they occur after the clef sign and at the beginning of each line of music. "Music Theory Workbook for Guitar Volume Two" covers learning all scales and their associated keys.

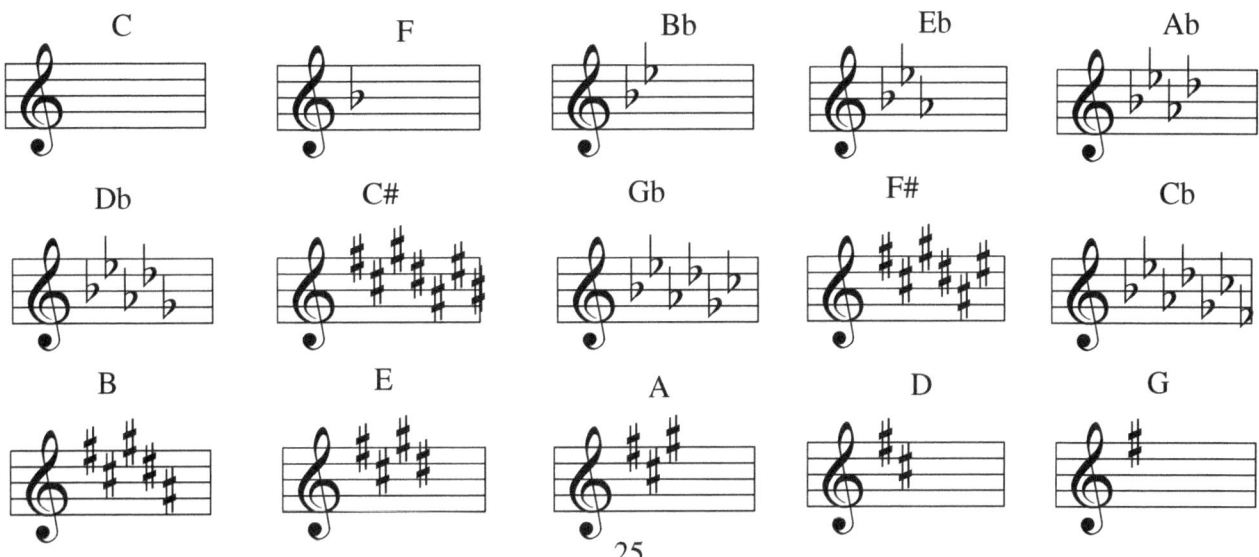

Whole steps and half steps are the basic building blocks for the major scale. The whole step equals two half steps. The distance between two notes is called an interval. For example the distance between C and D is a whole step. This is also called a major second interval. It is important to know intervals because chords are frequently named for the intervals in their internal structure. All two note interval combinations from the root of the major scale are listed below.

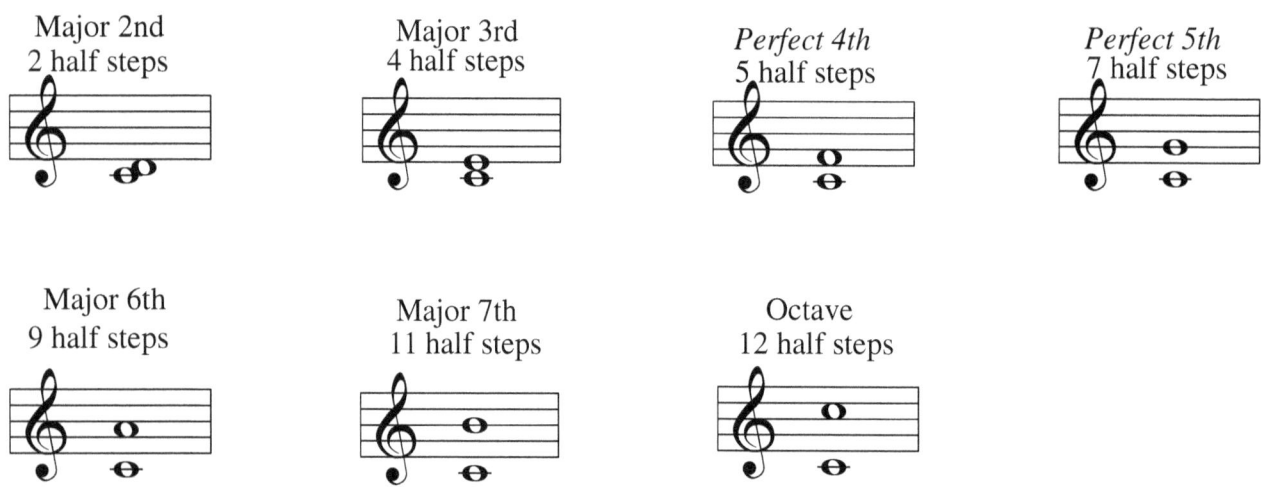

If we sharp any of these intervals we create an augmented interval. If we flat a major second, third, sixth, or seventh we create a minor interval. If we flat a perfect fourth, a fifth, or an octave, we get a diminished interval, and *if we double flat the major 7th we have a diminished 7th.* The following is a list of some of the more common augmented, minor and diminished intervals. These are explored in all keys with the "Basic Intervals" exercise on page 36.

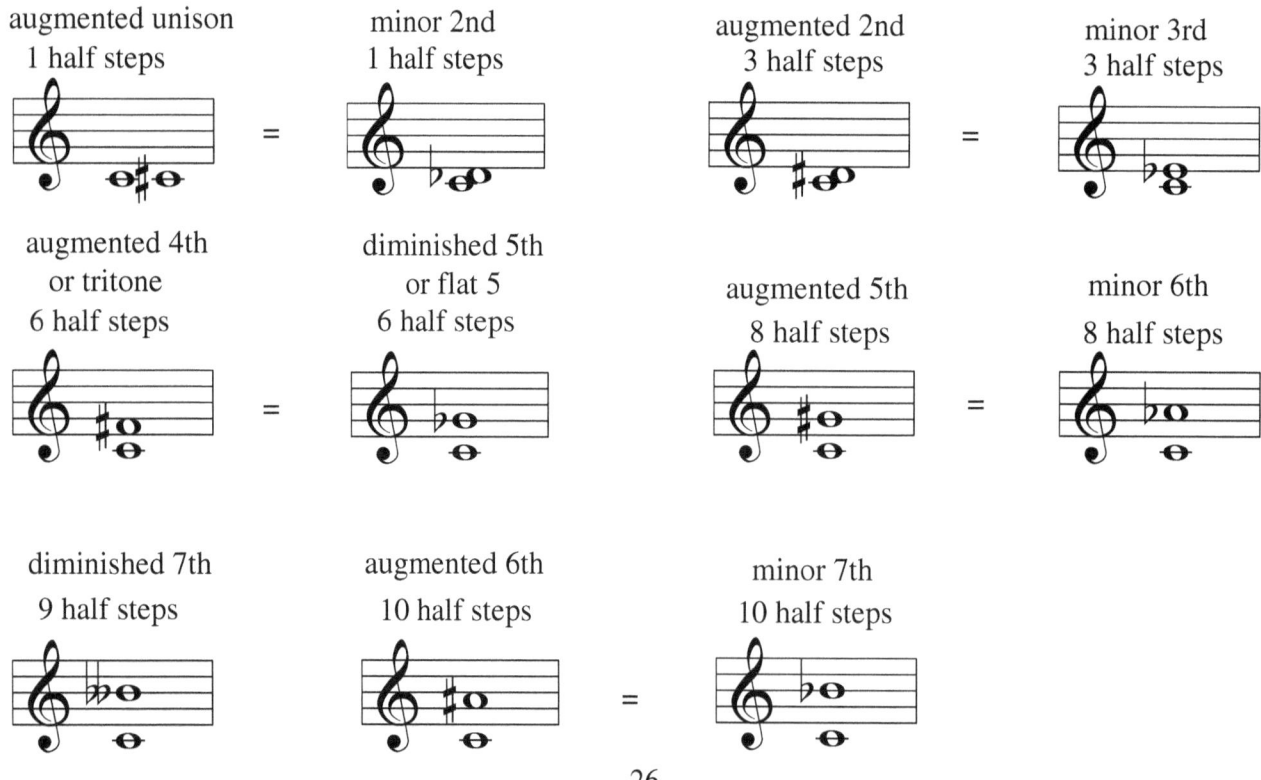

If we continue past the octave, intervals are given new names to show that they are more than an octave apart. The larger intervals exercise on page 17 of the "Music Theory Workbook for Guitar Volume One" covers these intervals. Here are a few examples.

An augmented interval may be written in different ways. A (+) may appear before the number, or a (#) or (aug).

If the interval is flatted it is usually indicated with a flat. Here are some of the common interval names you will need to know.

This knowledge of the chromatic scale, major scale and the construction of intervals are crucial tools to understanding the internal structure of chords.

So far we have discussed 2 note intervals, sometimes called diads. When we add one more note to our 2 note interval we create a chord. A chord can be a combination of any 3 or more notes played at the same time. Western music can build chords using a wide variety of intervals. One of the most common ways to build chords is to stack up diatonic 3rd intervals. For example if we took C in the key of C and stacked up 3rds we would get C, E, and G because all of those notes are in the key of C and are a 3rd apart. **These structures built in thirds are commonly referred to as triads and the C note is said to be the root of the chord**.

C Major Triad

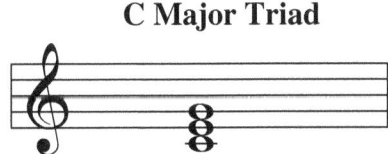

If we continue this process and build up diatonic triads above all the notes of C major we get the following 3 note structures.

Triads derived from stacking 3rds above a C major scale

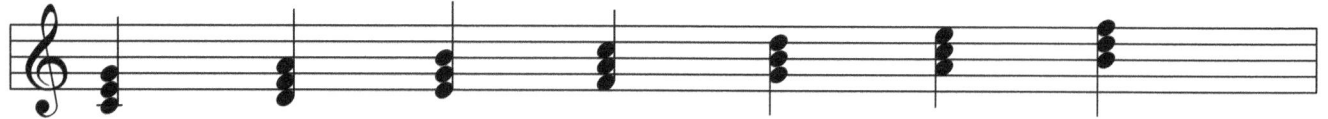

These seven chords have a specific internal structure. The first structure C, E, and G form what is called a major chord, if we measure the distance or interval between each note using our chromatic scale we can find the formula for building major chords. Between C and E is 4 half steps or a major third. Between E and G is 3 half steps or a minor third. Therefore to create a major chord we need to combine a major third on the bottom and a minor third on the top. You will notice that the chord starting on F and on G are also major chords. The exercise on page 37 covers major triads.

C major chord

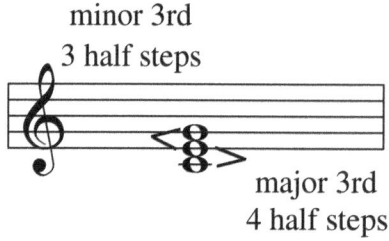

The second structure D, F, and A form what is called a minor chord. Using the chromatic scale once again we can find the formula for building minor chords. Between D and F is 3 half steps or a minor third. Between F and A is 4 half steps or a major third. Therefore to create a minor chord we need to combine a minor third on the bottom and a major third on the top. You will notice that the chord starting on E and on A are also minor chords. The exercise on page 19 of the "Music Theory Workbook for Guitar Volume One" covers minor triads.

D minor chord

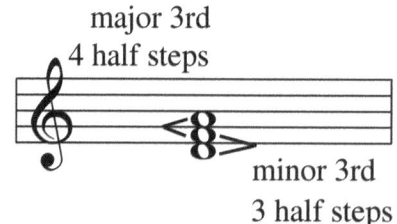

This leaves us with one last structure B, D, F which forms what is called a diminished chord. Using the same method we find that the distance between B and D is 3 half steps or a minor third. Between D and F is 3 half steps or a minor third. Therefore to create a diminished chord we need to combine a minor third on the bottom and a minor third on the top. The exercise on page 20 of the "Music Theory Workbook for Guitar Volume One" covers diminished triads.

B diminished chord

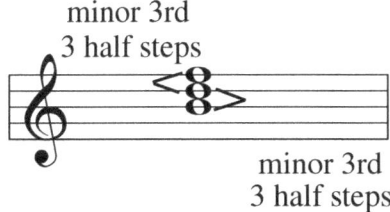

Below is a list of all the triads and their chord names. These chords are referred to as the diatonic triad or chords of a major key. You will see each of these chords labeled in many ways. C major could be shown as: C major, CMaj, C, CM, D minor could be shown as: D minor, Dmin, D-, Dm, B diminished could be shown as: B diminished, B dim, or B°.

They are also numbered sequentially which allows someone to refer to the D minor chord in the key of C, as a "II chord". Because many contemporary tunes are written using only the diatonic chords of a key it is a very common practice among musicians to learn the diatonic chords of every key using numbers and letters to aid in the memorization and quick learning of new songs. "Music Theory Workbook for Guitar Volume Three" covers learning these Diatonic Chords in all keys.

Diatonic chords of C Major

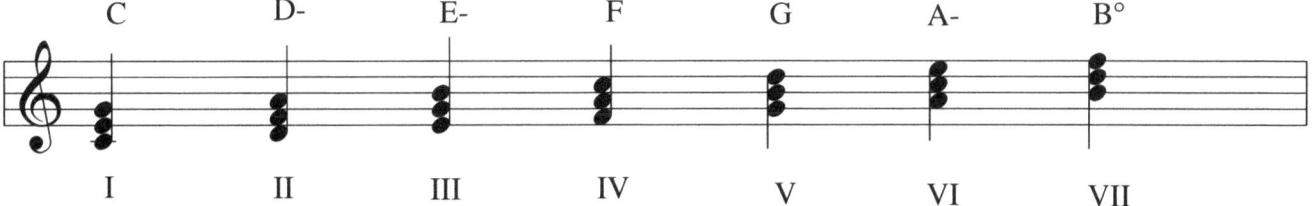

If we take the three types of chords learned so far and write them out with C as the root we come up with (ex. 1) C, E, G for a C major chord which is a major third stacked below a minor third, (ex. 2) C, Eb, G for a C minor chord which has just the opposite interval combination; a minor third stacked below a major third, and (ex. 3) C, Eb, Gb for a diminished chord which is two minor third intervals. You may notice that we have not yet discussed the combination of a major third and major third which is shown in (ex. 4) C, E, G#. This combination is called an augmented chord and is written as follows: C augmented, C aug, C+. The augmented chord can be found as a diatonic chord in other scales which are discussed in the "Music Theory Workbook for Guitar Volume Two." The exercise on page 21 of the "Music Theory Workbook for Guitar Volume One" covers augmented chords.

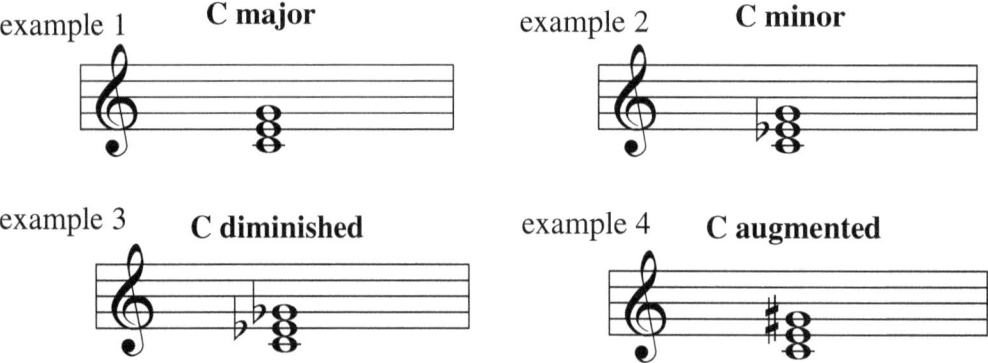

There are two more triad chord structures that are commonly found in contemporary music; the suspended 4th chord (sus 4) and the add 9th (add 9). The sus 4 is a triad in which the 4th has replaced the 3rd. This creates an unusual structure of 5 half steps or a 4th and 2 half steps or a major 2nd. The suspended chord can be a diatonic chord built on the 1st, 2nd, 3rd, 5th, or 6th degrees. It is common to see the suspended chord written as C4, C sus or C sus4. The add 9 replaces the 3rd with the second. The interval structure of this chord would be 2 half steps or a major 2nd and 5 half steps or a perfect 4th. The add 9 chord can be a diatonic chord build on the 1st, 2nd, 4th 5th or 6th degrees of the scale. The exercise on page 21 of the "Music Theory Workbook for Guitar Volume One" covers sus 4 and page 45 of the "Music Theory Workbook for Guitar Volume One" covers add 9 triads.

The notes of each chord are called the chord tones. For example, the chord tones of a C major chord are C, E, and G. It is also possible to build chords that contain more notes. The next most common chord type is a four note structure which is commonly referred to as a 7th chord. To build a 7th chord you add a note a third above the triads we have just discussed. If we add a major third above our C major triad we get C, E, G B

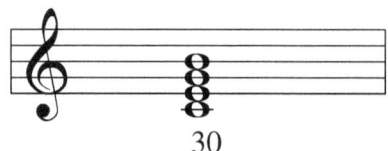

If we go back to our diatonic triads of C major and add a diatonic third above each chord we now have the diatonic 7th chords of the key of C major.

7th Chords derived from C major scale

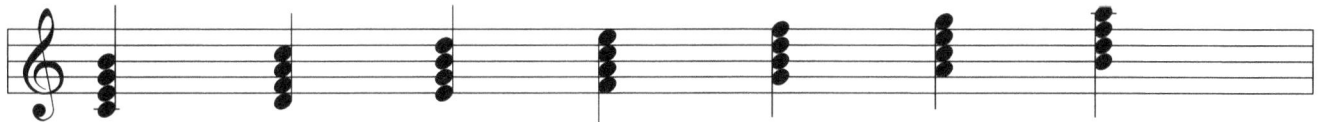

These seven 7th chords structures have a specific internal structure just as our triads did. The first structure (C, E, G and B) contains the triad C, E and G plus another major third up to B. This structure is called a major 7th chord. If we again measure the distance or interval between each note using our chromatic scale we can find the formula for building major 7th chords. Between C and E is 4 half steps or a major third, between E and G is 3 half steps or a minor third, G to B is 4 half steps or a major third. **Therefore to create a major 7th chord we need to combine a major third on the bottom and a minor third in the middle and a major third on the top**. You will notice that the chord starting on F is also a major 7th chord. The exercise on page 24 of the "Music Theory Workbook for Guitar Volume One" covers major 7th chords.

C major 7th chord

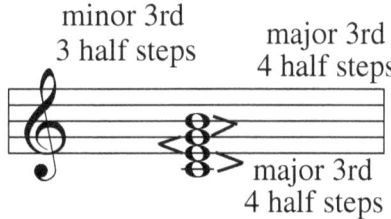

The second structure (D, F, A and C), forms what is called a minor 7th chord. Using the chromatic scale once again, we can find the formula for building minor 7th chords. Between D and F is 3 half steps or a minor third. Between F and A is 4 half steps or a major third; between A and C is 3 half steps or a minor third. **Therefore to create a minor 7th chord we need to combine a minor third on the bottom and a major third in the middle and a minor third on the top**. You will notice that the chord starting on E and on A are also minor 7th chords. The exercise on page 25 of the "Music Theory Workbook for Guitar Volume One" covers minor 7th chords.

D minor 7th

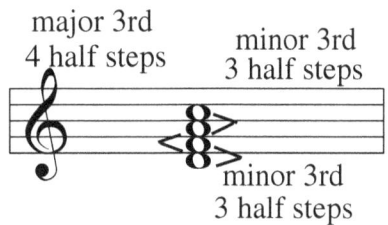

The third new structure G, B, D and F forms a dominant 7th chord. Using the chromatic scale we can find the formula for building dominant 7th chords. Between G and B is 4 half steps or a major third, between B and D is 3 half steps or a minor third, between D and F is 3 half steps or a minor third. **Therefore to create a dominant 7th chord we need to combine a major third on the bottom and a minor third in the middle and a minor third on the top**. Only one dominant seventh chord can appear naturally within any major key. The exercise on page 26 of the "Music Theory Workbook for Guitar Volume One" covers dominant 7th chords.

G dominant 7th chord

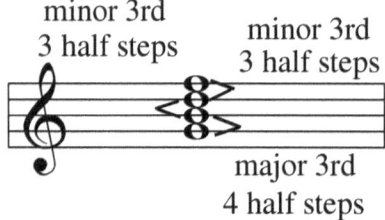

The last structure B, D, F and A form what is called a minor 7 flat 5, also referred to as the "half diminished" chord. Using the chromatic scale we can find the formula for building minor 7 flat 5 chords. Between B and D is 3 half steps or a minor third, between D and F is 3 half steps or a minor third and between F and A is 4 half steps or a major third. **Therefore to create a minor 7b5 chord we need to combine a minor third on the bottom and a minor third in the middle and a major third on the top**. The minor 7b5, like the dominant 7th, happens only once in diatonic 7th chords of a major key. The exercise on page 28 of the "Music Theory Workbook for Guitar Volume One" covers minor 7b5 chords.

B minor 7 flat 5 chord

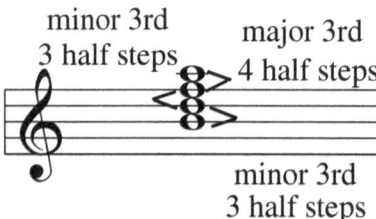

The 7th chords can be organized in the same manner as our triads were. Below is a list of the diatonic 7th chords of a major key. These chords again can be labeled in many ways: C major 7 could be shown as C major 7, CMaj7, C∆7, CM7. D minor 7 could be shown as D minor 7, Dmin 7, D-7, Dm7. G dominant 7th could be shown as G dominant, G dom7, or G7. B minor 7th flat 5 can be shown as B minor 7b5, Bmin7b5, and B-7b5.

The same numbering system applies for the 7th chords as for the triads.

Here are the chords listed sequentially with their chord names and degrees.

Diatonic 7th chords of C Major

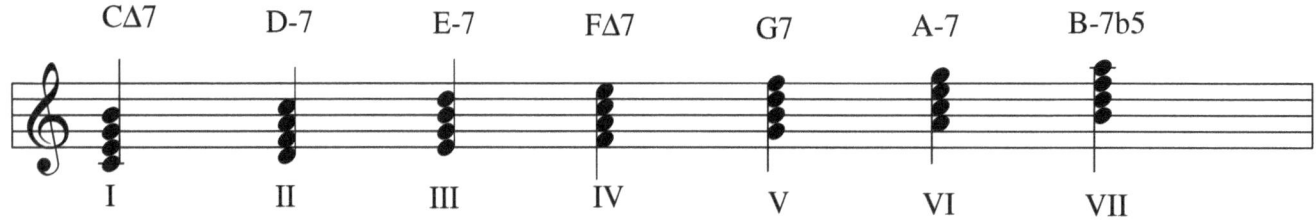

Most styles of music generally use triads or 7th chords with or without tensions. For instance, folk music gravitates toward triads while jazz tends to use more 7th chords and even more complicated structures.

If we extend the idea of adding more notes to chords by extending up another 3rd above our 7th tone we create 9th chords. Therefore CΔ7 (C, E, G, B) becomes CΔ79 (C, E, G, B, D), the interval formula would be maj3, min3, maj3, min3. The 9th is a tension, not a chord tone. A tension in contemporary music is a non chord tone which adds color to our basic triads and 7th chords.

The method of using intervals by calculating half steps gets very time consuming as the chord structures get larger and larger. **There is a faster way to calculate which notes are contained in any chord but this requires that you first memorize the major scale.** If we go back and look at our C major scale we can see that to find for example, a major 7 chord which is C, E, G, and B we need only to think the 1, 3, 5, 7 degrees of the C major scale. To add on a tension like the 9th we simply add the 2nd degree of the C major scale which is a D. When the 2nd is placed above the 7th it is called the 9th. We need only to add the 2nd degree of C (which we have learned is the same note as the 9th).

Δ9th chord

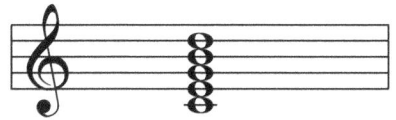

If we use the major scale as our reference point in figuring out chord tones we only need to know the formula for each chord type. For example: a C-7 chord would be C, Eb, G, Bb which would be 1, b3, 5 and b7 in the key of C. Therefore by memorizing the structure of each chord and altering the notes from the major scale we can quickly find the correct notes for any chord. Below is a list of the triads and seventh chords and their relationship to a C major scale.

triad chords
major   (1 3 5)
minor   (1 b3 5)
diminished (1 b3 b5)
augmented (1 3 #5)
sus4   (1 4 5)

7th chords
Δ7   (1 3 5 7)
-7   (1 b3 5 b7)
7   (1 3 5 b7)
-7b5   (1 b3 b5 b7)
°7   (1 b3 b5 bb7)
-Δ7   (1 b3 5 7)
7sus4 (1 4 5 b7)
Δ7#5   (1 3 #5 7)
7#5   (1 3 #5 b7)
Δ7#11 (1 3 #4 7)
7#11   (1 3 #4 b7)
6   (1 3 5 6)
-6   (1 b3 5 6)

When we add even more tensions to our triads or seventh chords we simply have to add the appropriate note from our reference major scale. For example: Cdom9 would be C, E, G, Bb, D or 1, 3, 5, b7, and 9th degrees of a C major scale. Tensions are applied in the exercises starting on page 38 of the "Music Theory Workbook for Guitar Volume One."

C reference scale

flat the (B) for b7

1	2	3	4	5	6	7	1
	or		or		or		
	9		11		13		

In the "Music Theory Workbook for Guitar Volume One" there is a review of the available tensions for each chord type. There is also a brief overview of how each chord type is used is also included.

The chord diagrams used in this book are explained below. When completing the exercises you do not have to put the name of the notes within each black circle.

chord diagrams

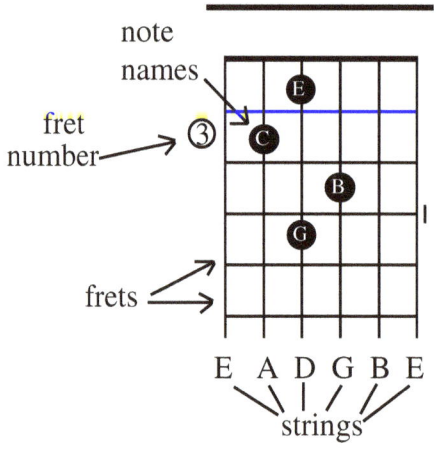

It must be mentioned that the guitar is a transposing instrument sounding an octave (12 half steps) lower than written. Therefore middle C on a piano appears as the C one ledger line below the staff while the actual sound of middle C on the guitar is 1st fret on the B string. All staff notation in this book is transposed.

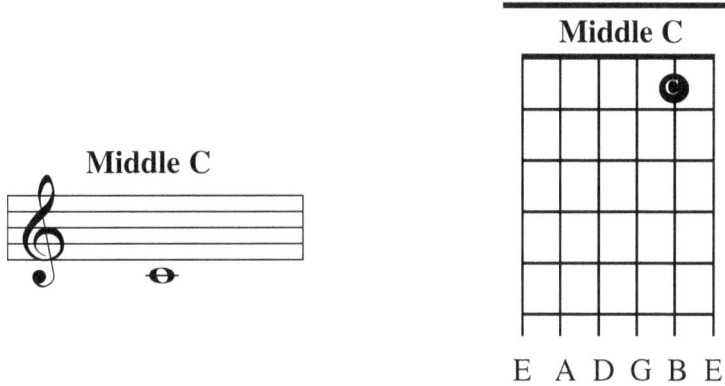

Therefore the open strings on the guitar would be written as follows:

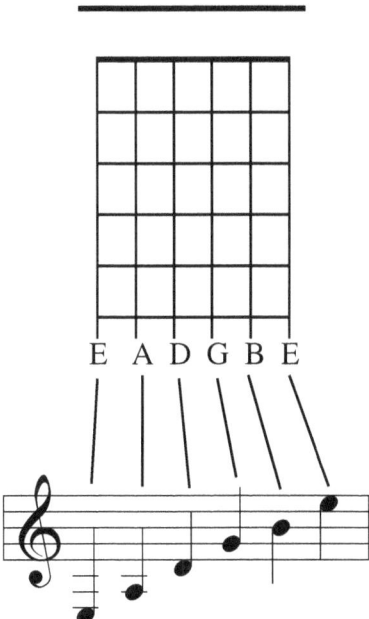

Basic Intervals

Example

perfect 5 | major 7 | perfect 4 | major 3

major 2 | augmented unison | minor 2 | augmented 2

minor 3 | tritone | augmented 4 | flat 5

diminished 5 | augmented 5 | minor 6 | diminished 7

augmented 6 | minor 7 | perfect 5 | major 7

major 6 | perfect 4 | major 3 | major 2

augmented unison | minor 2 | augmented 2 | minor 3

tritone | augmented 4 | flat 5 | diminished 5

Major Triads

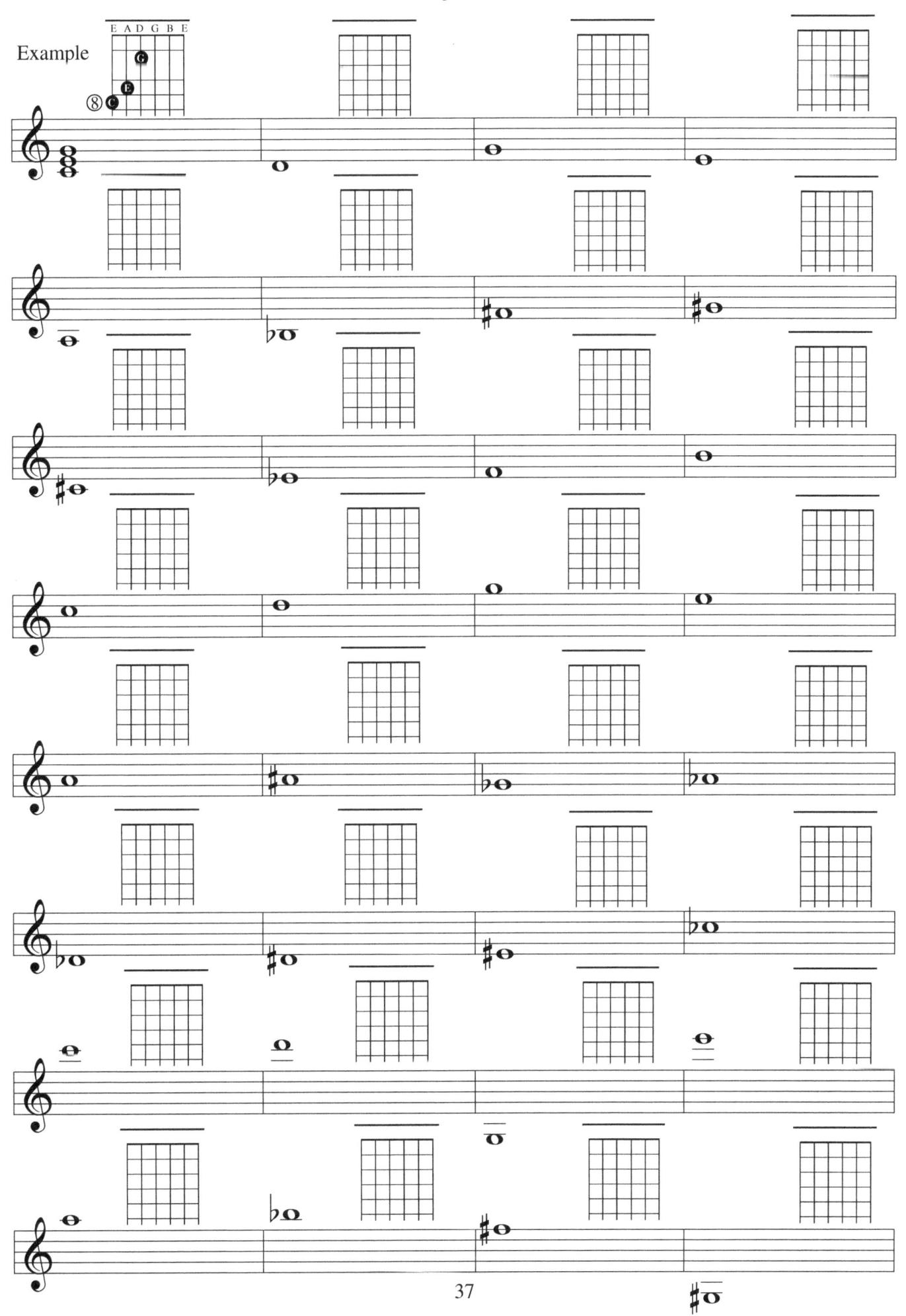

Chord Tones and Tensions
Dominant 7th
7
Chord Tones 1 3 5 b7
Tensions b9 9 #9 #11 #5 13

Chords with Tensions

Below is a list of the chord tones and tensions for a dominant chord. Once again there is no limit to how many tensions can be in a chord, but because the guitar has only 6 strings we are limited to 6 notes.

The chord tones and tensions for C7 are as follows:

1   3   5   b7   b9   9   #9   #11   #5 or b13   13

All the tensions that we learn for each chord can be used as a substitute for the basic chord type. Dominant chords have many possibilities for adding and combining tensions. For instance if we have a C7 chord we could substitute C7#11 or C7#9b13 etc. Theoretically any combination is possible. Usually tensions are not combined that are a half step apart. For example, you usually don't have a dominant chord which contains "b9" and natural 9. Also most of these half step possibilities don't lay well on the guitar.

Although any tension combination is possible there are common situations where certain tensions are preferred over others. When a dominant chord resolves up a fourth to a major chord i.e. C7 to FΔ7 it is common to use natural tensions 9 or 13. When a dominant chord resolves up a fourth to a minor chord i.e. C7 to F-7 it is common to use the altered tensions b9, #9, b13. The reason C7 to FΔ7 uses natural tension is that the 9 and 13 (in this case, on C7 that would be D and A), are diatonic to the F major scale therefore creating an expectation of an impending major resolution. On the other hand if C7 resolves to an F minor chord, the altered tensions (in this case, on C7 they would be Db, Eb, Ab) are commonly used because they are found in various F minor scales. Db and Ab could be from the F harmonic minor scale and Eb from the natural minor scale. There are of course many other F minor scales that these three notes are found in. You can find many examples of these different tension combinations in the progression section found at the end of "Chord workbook for Guitar Volume One."

Dominant 7 #11 b13 Chords

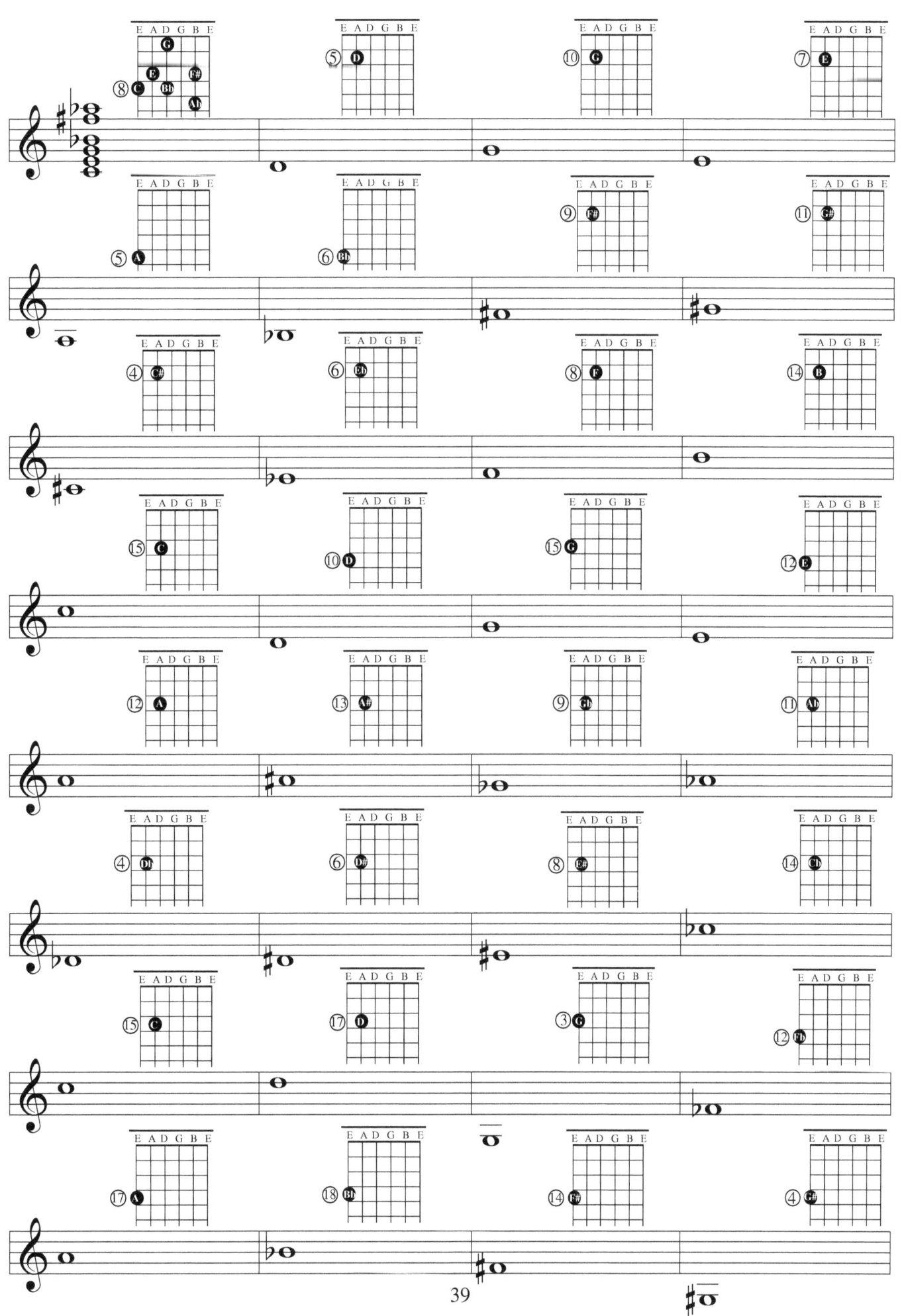

ANSWER PAGES

The following pages contain the answers to the exercises found on pages 36, 37, and 39. Keep in mind that because the same note can appear in many different places on the guitar neck, there can be more than one correct answer to each exercise. If you would like a complete list of answers for each exercise you can download the alternative answers at www.muse-eek.com The answers found on the following pages and on the alternative answer pages on the muse-eek website limit the range to five frets on the guitar fretboard. Five frets is the most comfortable and practical range for most guitarist's hands. There are of course even more possible answers but they would use uncomfortably large stretches or totally unplayable combinations.

Muse Eek hosts a secure area of their website for customers who own their books. This secure area provides additional resources for the serious student. At this time there is no additional charge for this information; just register and receive a password to enter it. This secure section is an ongoing project provided by Muse Eek, containing extra help files, video clips, and other educational information.

Our goal at Muse Eek is to provide the best distance learning resource for music, and any suggestions to augment or improve the site are welcomed. Please e-mail us at info@muse-eek.com

Basic Intervals Answers

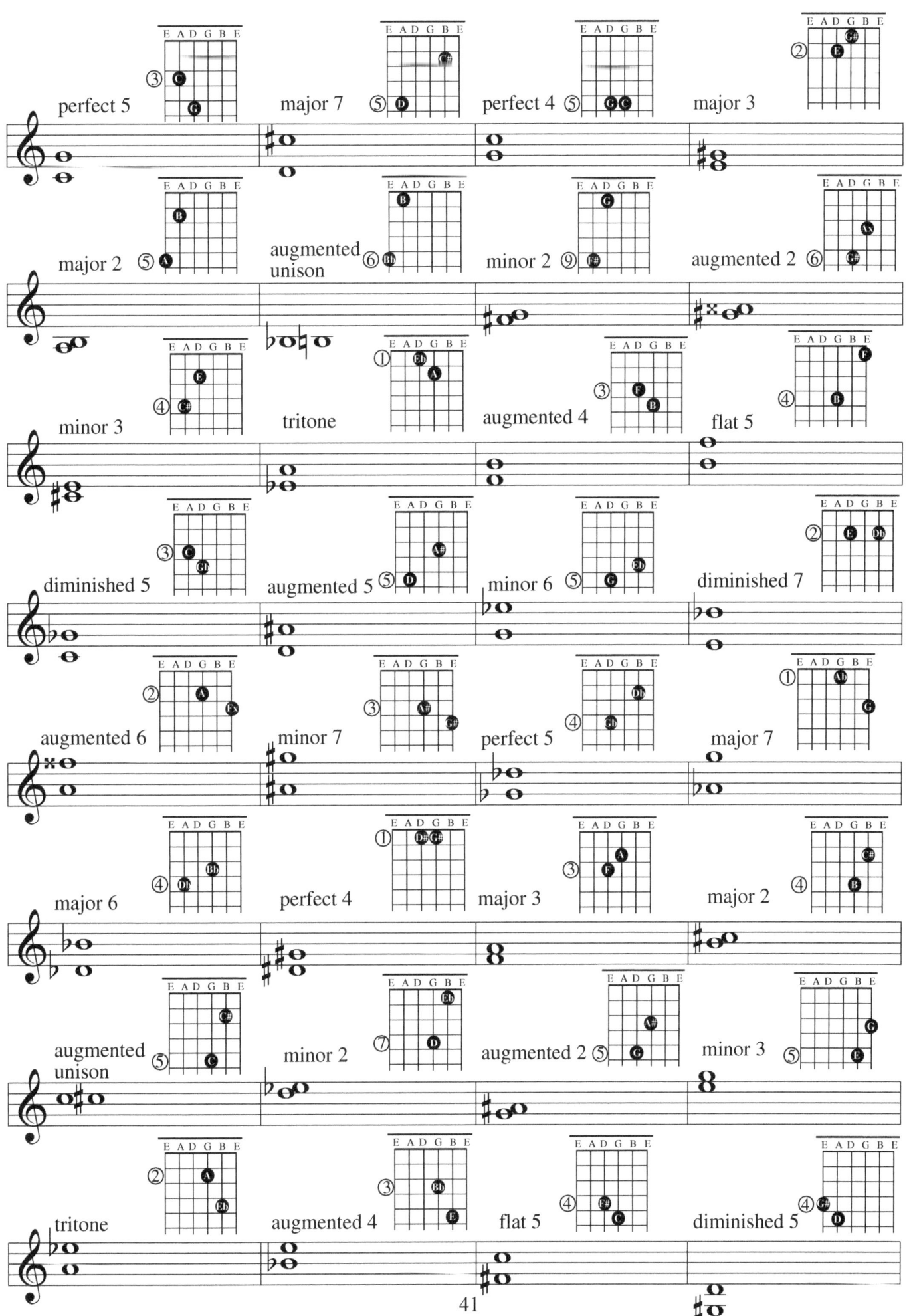

Major Triads Answers

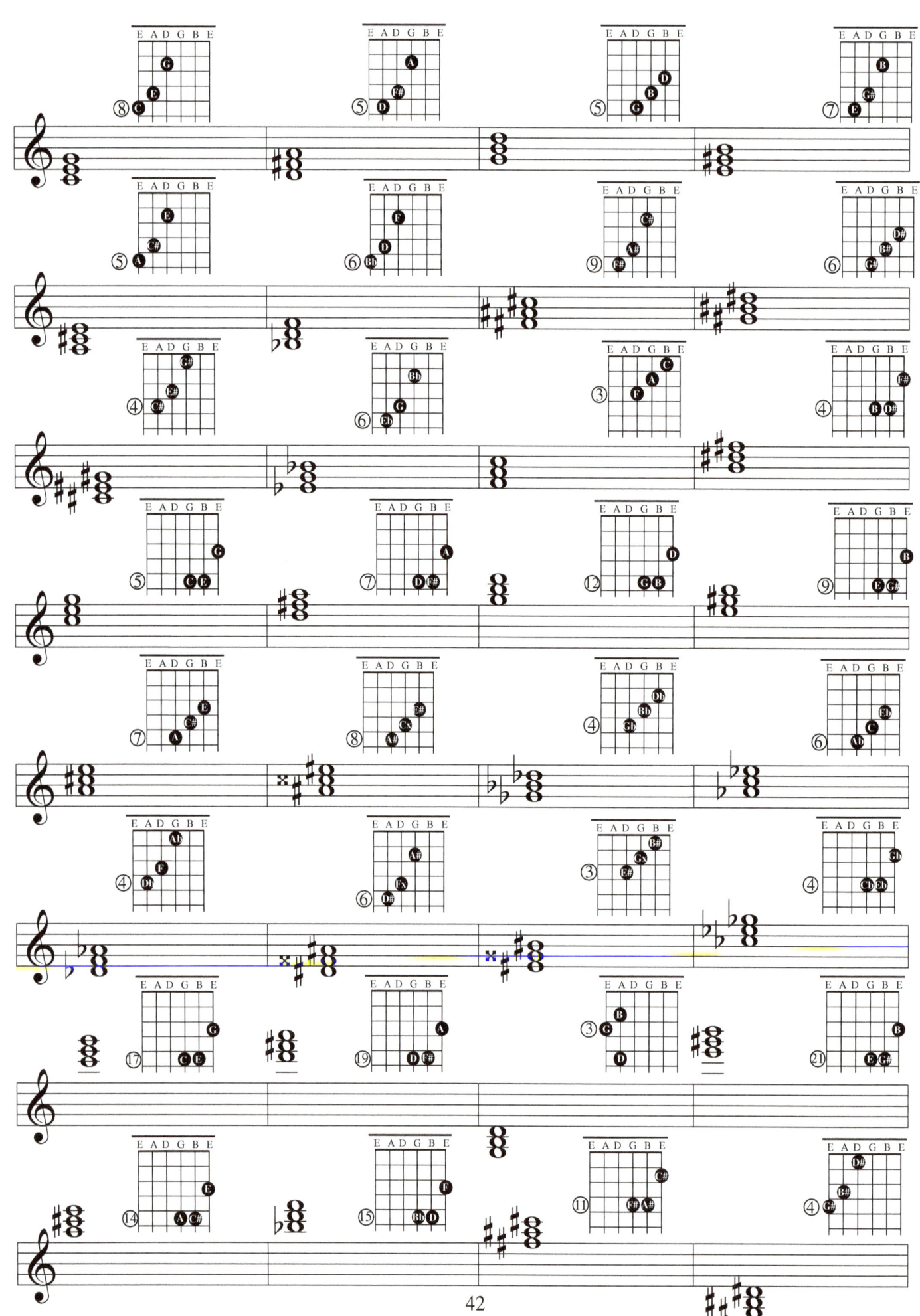

Dominant 7 #11 b13 Chords Answers

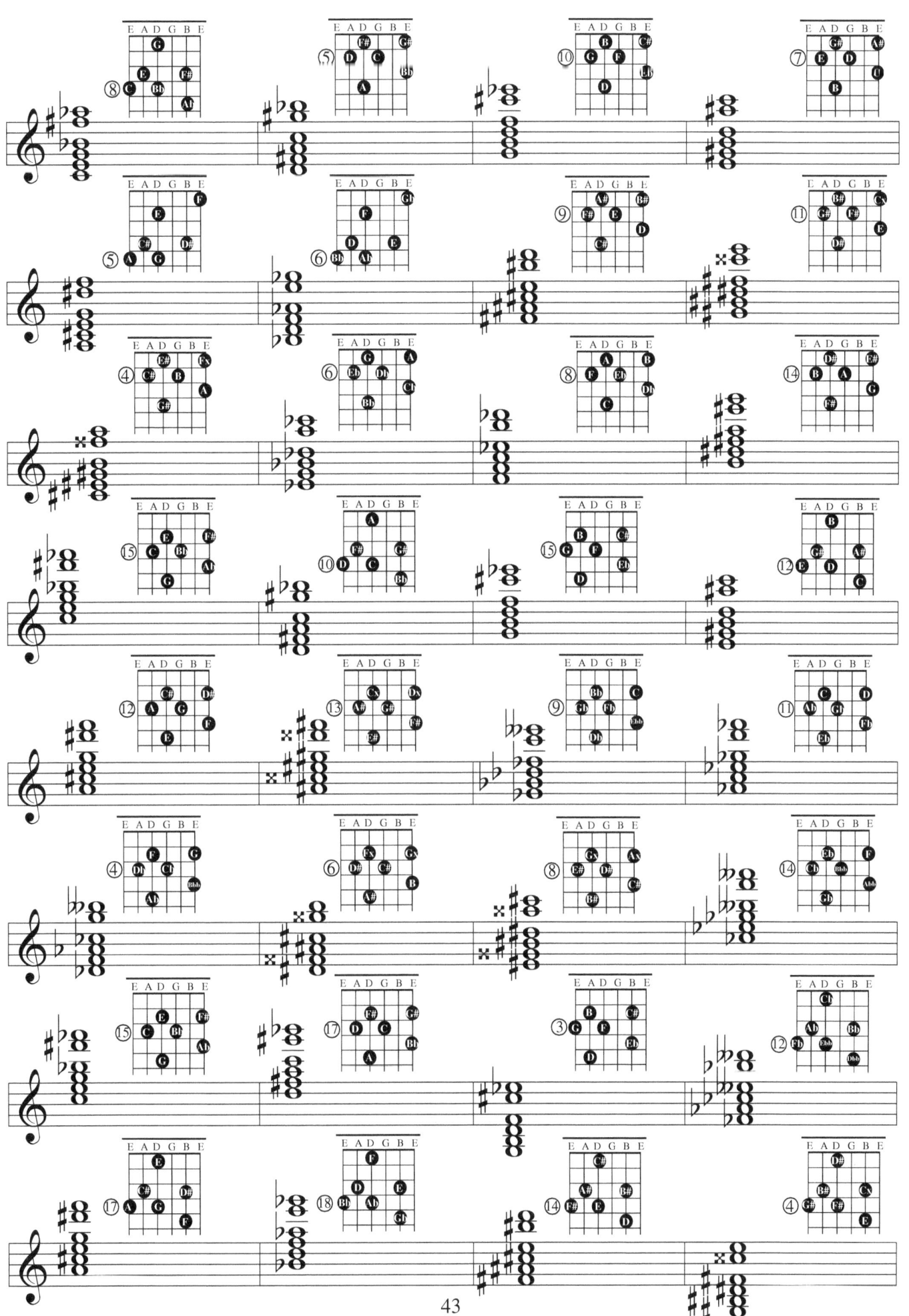

Scales

The scales section of this book is divided up into four sections.

1. Pages 45-46 contain an excerpt from "Music Theory Workbook for Guitar Volume Two." This excerpt discusses the structure of a major and dorian scale along with suggested chord progressions for applying these scales. Audio files for these progressions can be found on the Muse-eek.com website.

2. Pages 47-54 contain exercise excerpts from "Music Theory Workbook for Guitar Volume Two." These exercises help a student learn a major and dorian scale in all keys.

3. Pages 55-62 contain the answers to the exercises found on pages 47-54. **Page 63** contains a blank worksheet for a student to use for extra exercise work.

4. Pages 64-71 contain a short discussion and the fingering for the major and dorian scales. The fingering for the pentatonic and blues scales are also included. More fingerings for other scales can be found on the internet at the "Music Workshop" located at www.arnoldjazz.com

It is also recommended that you apply the scales learned here to the modal sequencing section of this book located on pages 87-90.

The most important thing you can remember as a guitarist when working through this section is that you want to learn each scale as the notes or degrees and not as fingering patterns.

So here we Go!

The Major scale is just one of 22 scales or modes that are commonly used in contemporary music. Pages 45-46 will show you how two of these 22 scales are built. It is recommended that you work on each new scale presented in 3 ways. First, digest the information presented about the structure of the scale, then move to the corresponding section and write out the scale in all keys. Then use the progressions to work on improvising. You will find the fingering for each scale on pages 65-71. When you are ready, transpose these progressions to all keys. Be creative and try to come up with other chord progressions that would work with each scale presented. **Be Patient and allow yourself time.** This is a rigorous course of study and should take the average student a year to complete, with consistent application. You may find that you start to run into chords that you don't know as you get into more complicated scales.

By knowing their interval patterns you can play any scale. Pages 45-46 gives you the interval patterns for Major and Dorian. There are a couple of possible ways to memorize the structure of a scale. The method on page 24 of memorizing a scale's interval pattern will certainly help you figure out any scale. Once you have memorized the major scales you could also use an alternate method to help you learn the other scales: If you think of what alterations a scale has in comparison to C major i.e. (C Dorian has a flatted 3rd and 7th, you will be able to relate each new scale to a scale you already know. Once you have memorized the 7 modes of major: Major, Dorian, Phrygian, Lydian, Mixolydian, Aeolian and Locrian you can use these scales to help you memorize other scales. For instance if you want to learn a Dorian b2 scale just flat the second degree of the Dorian scale and you have your new scale. Learning scales using this method will help you master scales quickly because they are relating back to a scale you know while keeping the root the same. You will find all of these scales with corresponding exercises in the "Music Theory Workbook for Guitar Volume Two."

Many people learn scales like the Dorian by relating it to its parent major scale. (D Dorian has the same notes as C Major). I don't recommend using this method as your sole means of memorizing scales. Having to constantly relate back to another scale to figure out the scale you need is time consuming and gets crazy when you have many chords in a progression. It also goes against how you naturally hear music. For example if you have a D minor vamp you will *hear* this vamp in D minor, so why *think* in C major? Conversely, there are places where you can group a bunch of chords together and play one scale over all chords. For instance if you had a progression like:

$$|: C\Delta 7 \ / \ A\text{-}7 \ / \ | \ D\text{-}7 \ / \ G7 \ / :|$$

You could just play a C major scale over all the chords because the chord scale for each chord would all have the same notes as C Major and the chord progression is combined in a way that makes you hear C major as the key center.

With the two scales presented in this book, you will be given its interval pattern, the alterations from a major scale, and common chord progressions that this scale works over.

Use this work section two ways: Write out and play each scale from its root in one position, and then up and down each string. It is also recommended that you use the blank notation page found on page 63 to write out each scale starting from the lowest fretted note of each string.

Our first scale as previously discussed is the Major scale which is a seven note scale whose interval pattern is: whole step, whole step, half step, whole step, whole step, whole step, half step. It is used over a Major, Major 7 or Major 6th chord. A C Major scale contains the notes C,D,E,F,G,A,B. If we play this scale up and down the A string it looks like this:

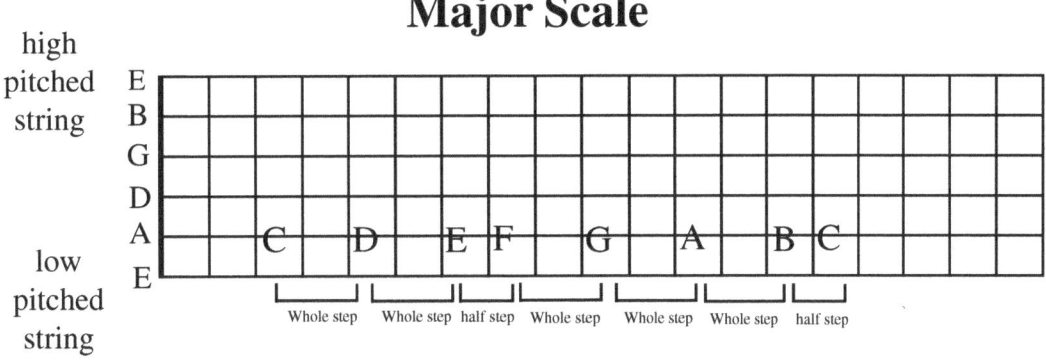

Along with the chord progression above, use these chord sequences to help you apply the major scale.

$$|: C\Delta 7 \ / \ / \ / \ | \ D\text{-}7 \ / \ / \ / :|$$

$$|: E\text{-}7 \ / \ / \ / \ | \ D\text{-}7 \ / \ / \ / \ | \ C\Delta 7 \ / \ / \ / \ | \ C\Delta 7 \ / \ / \ / :|$$

All the chords used for the progressions in this book are diatonic to each scale used. For instance, E-7, D-7 and C∆7 chords in the previous example can all be found by stacking up notes in 3rds above each root i.e.. E,G,B,D, forms an E-7 chord, D,F,A,C forms a D-7, and C,E,G,B forms a C∆7 chord. Volume 3 of the "Music Theory Workbook for Guitar" covers the diatonic chords of all scales, furthering an understanding of which chords are commonly grouped together.

Dorian Scale

The Dorian scale is a seven note scale whose interval pattern is: whole step, half step, whole step, whole step, whole step, half step, whole step. It is used over a minor 7th or dominant 7th sus4 chord. A C Dorian scale would contain the notes C,D,Eb,F,G,A,Bb. If we play this scale up and down the A string it looks like this:

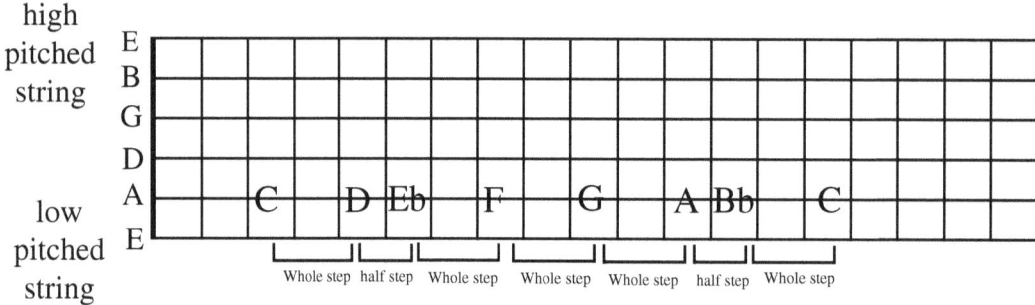

It is sometimes easier to think of the Dorian scale as a major scale where the 3rd and the 7th have been flatted rather than memorizing the interval pattern. It should also be pointed out that if we play a Bb major scale starting on the 2nd degree (C) we will be playing a C Dorian scale (C,D,Eb,F,G,A,Bb,C).

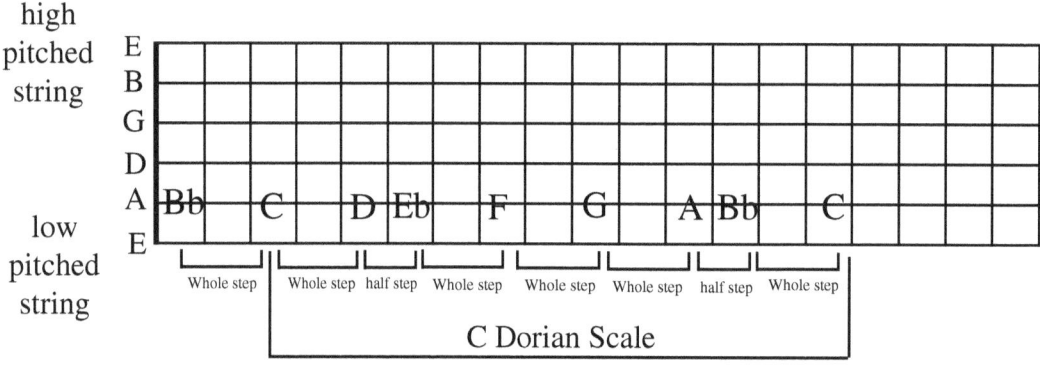

It is important to know each scale in two ways:

First, memorize its interval pattern or what alterations it has in comparison to C major. In this case, C Dorian has a flatted 3rd and 7th. You want to develop the ability to hear Dorian as its own key. The following progressions give you an example of hearing C Dorian as the key center. Notice that all the chords used in these progressions are diatonic to the key of C Dorian.

$$|: C\text{-}7\ /\ /\ /\ :| \qquad\qquad |: C\text{-}7\ /\ /\ /\ |\ Bb\triangle 7\ /\ D\text{-}7\ /\ :|$$

Second, memorize which major scale a particular mode comes from. In this case C Dorian is the 2nd degree of Bb major. This second method allows you to group similar scales together. For the following progression you could just play a Bb major scale over all the chords because the chord scale for each chord would have the same notes as a Bb Major and the chord progression is combined in a way that makes you hear Bb major as the key center.

$$|: Bb\triangle 7\ /\ /\ /\ |\ C\text{-}7\ /\ F7\ /\ :|$$

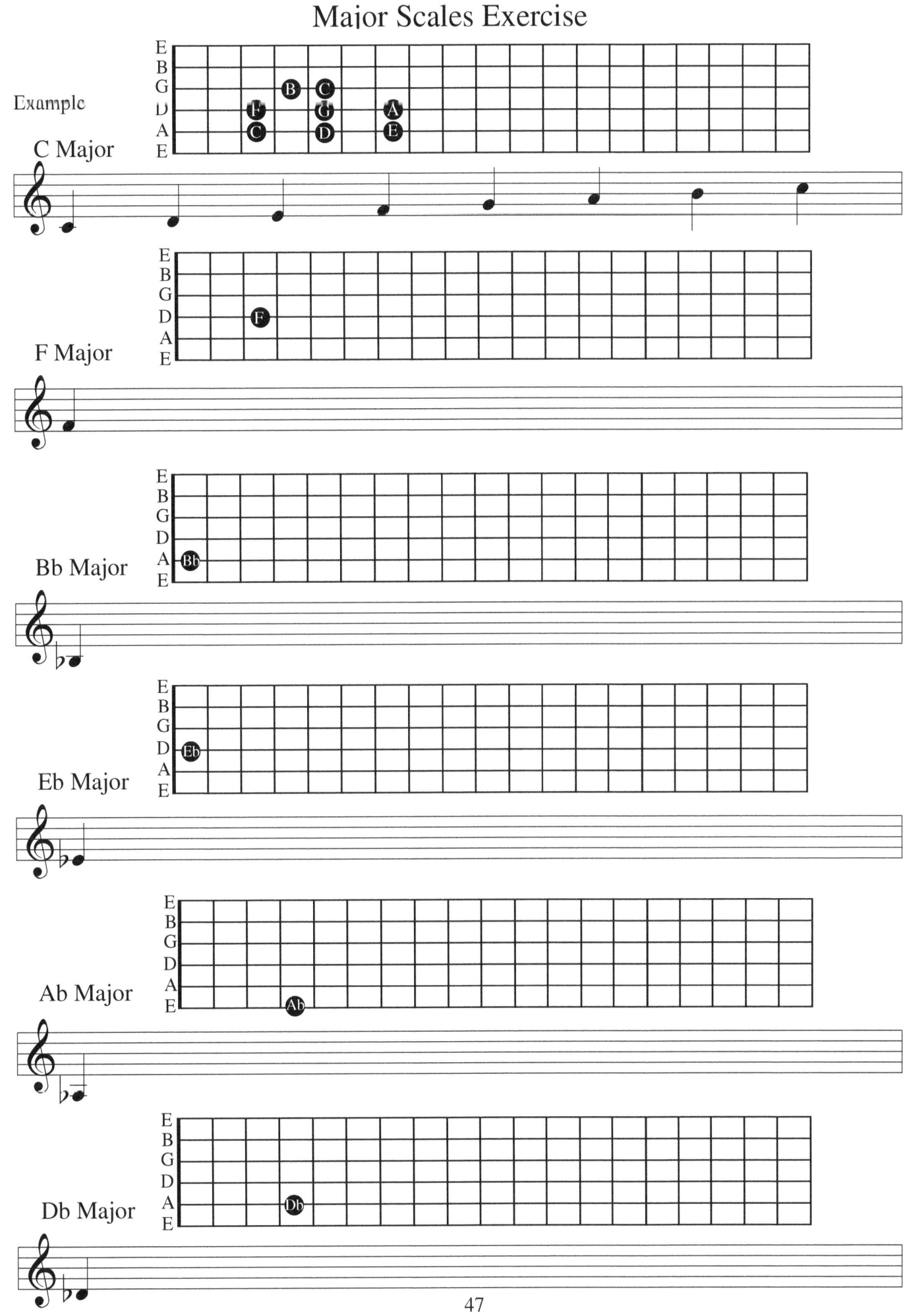

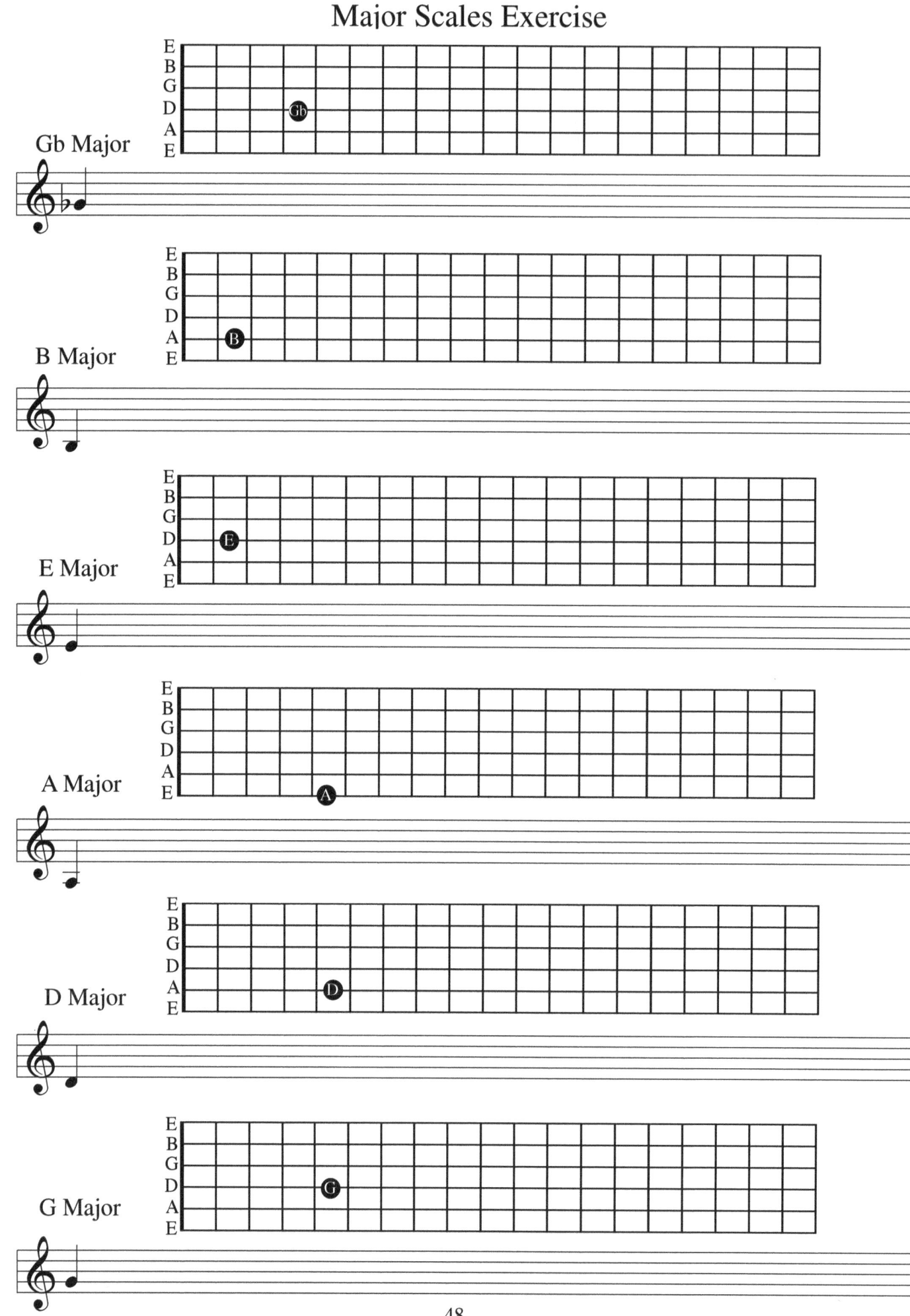

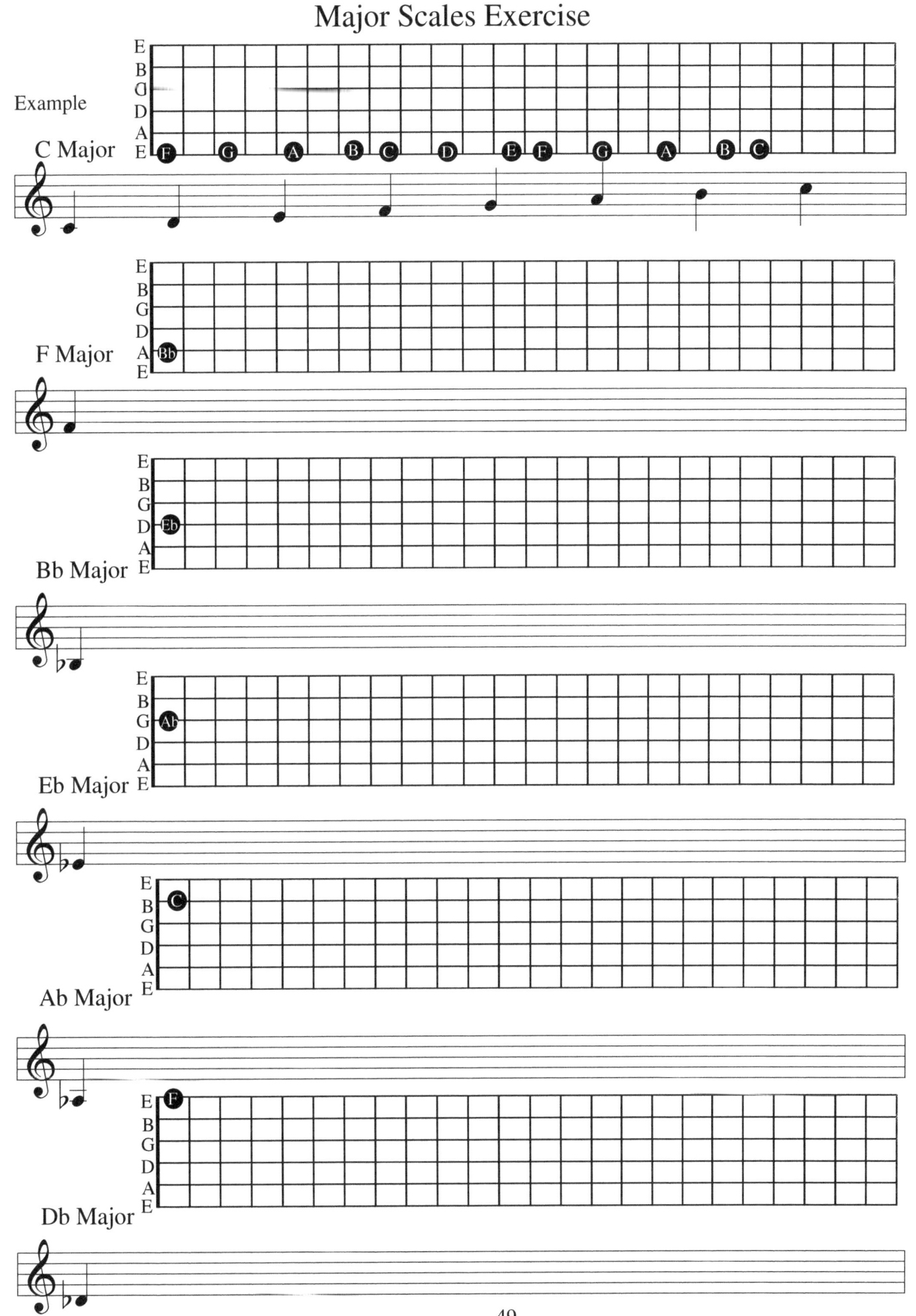

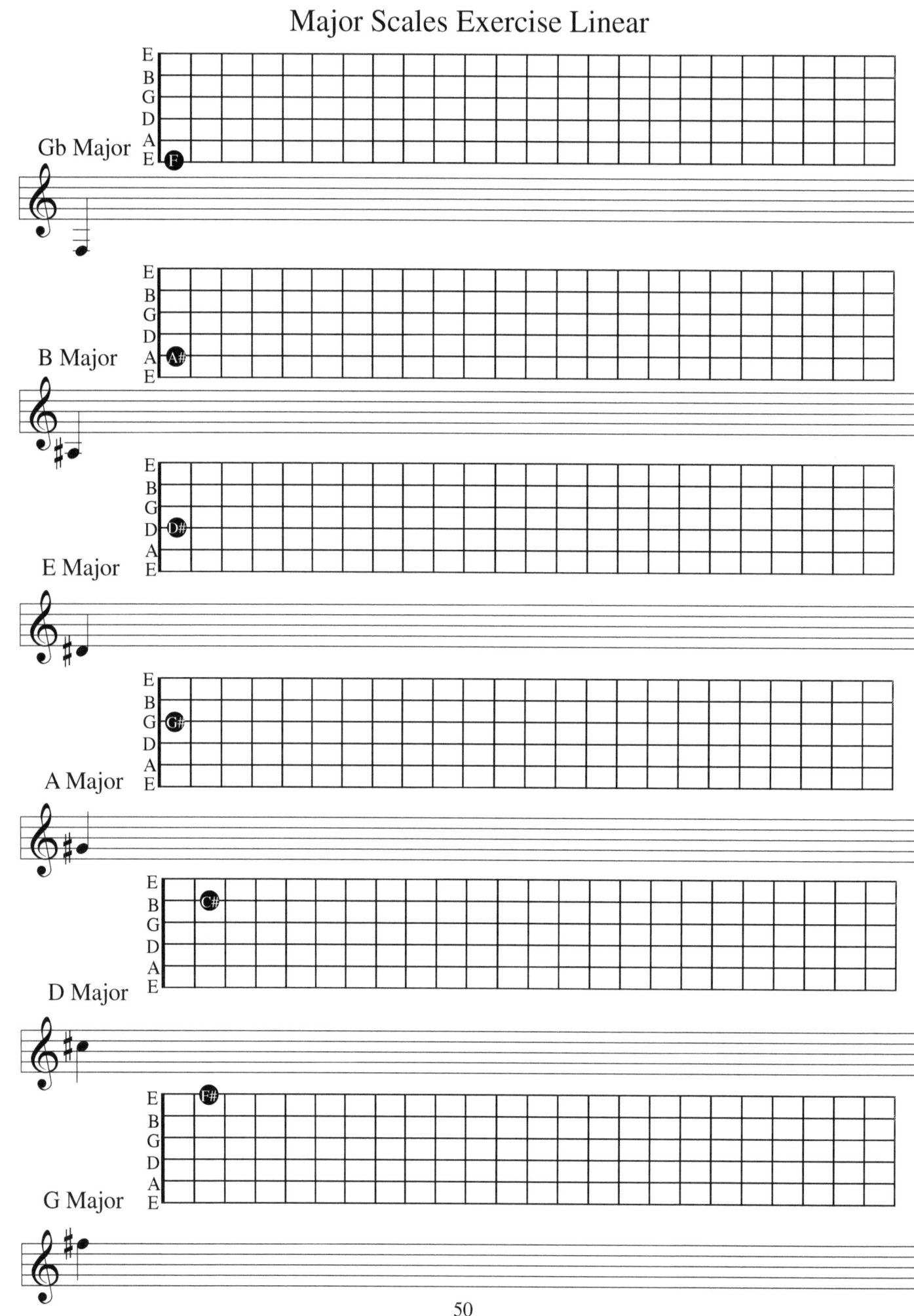

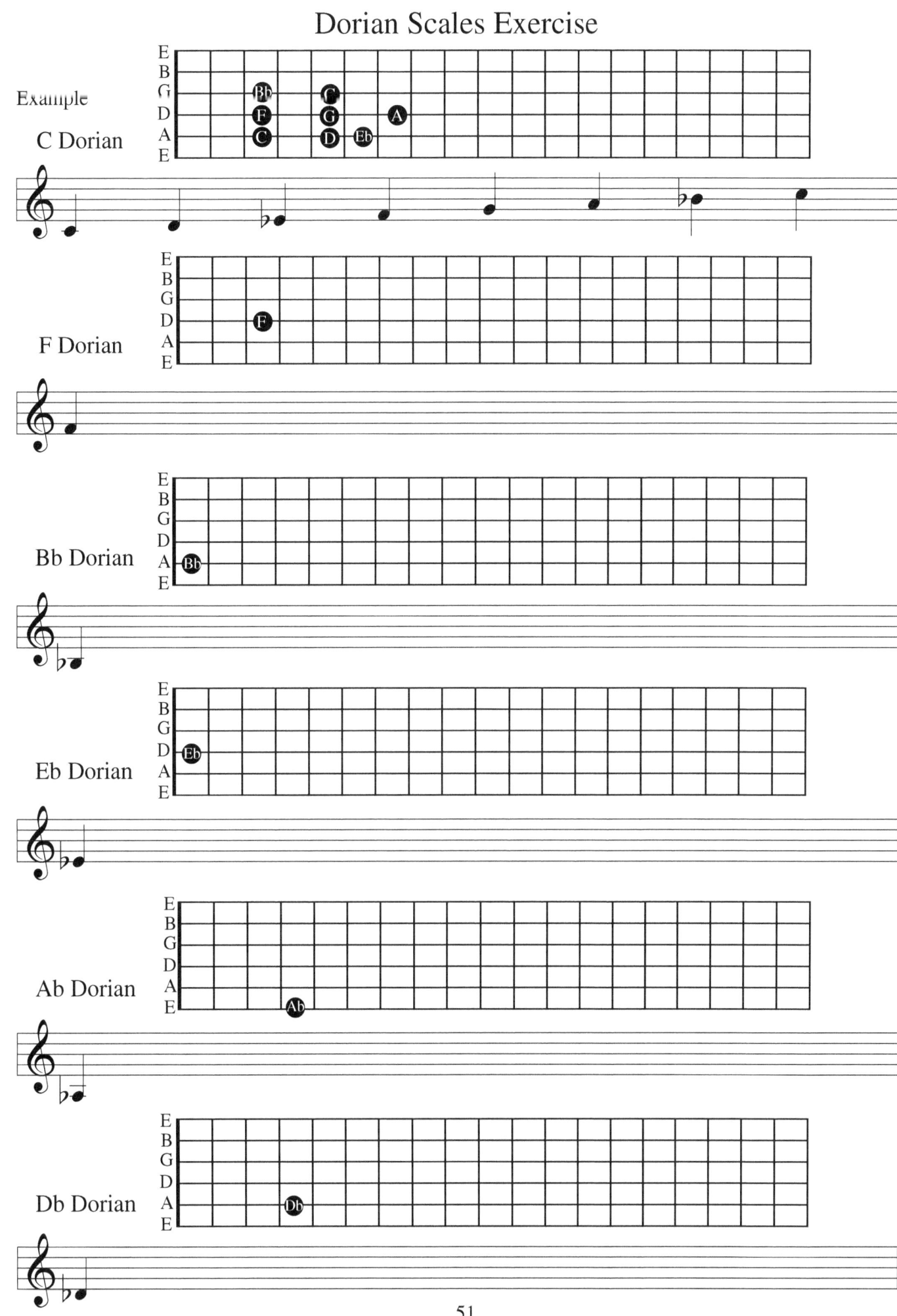

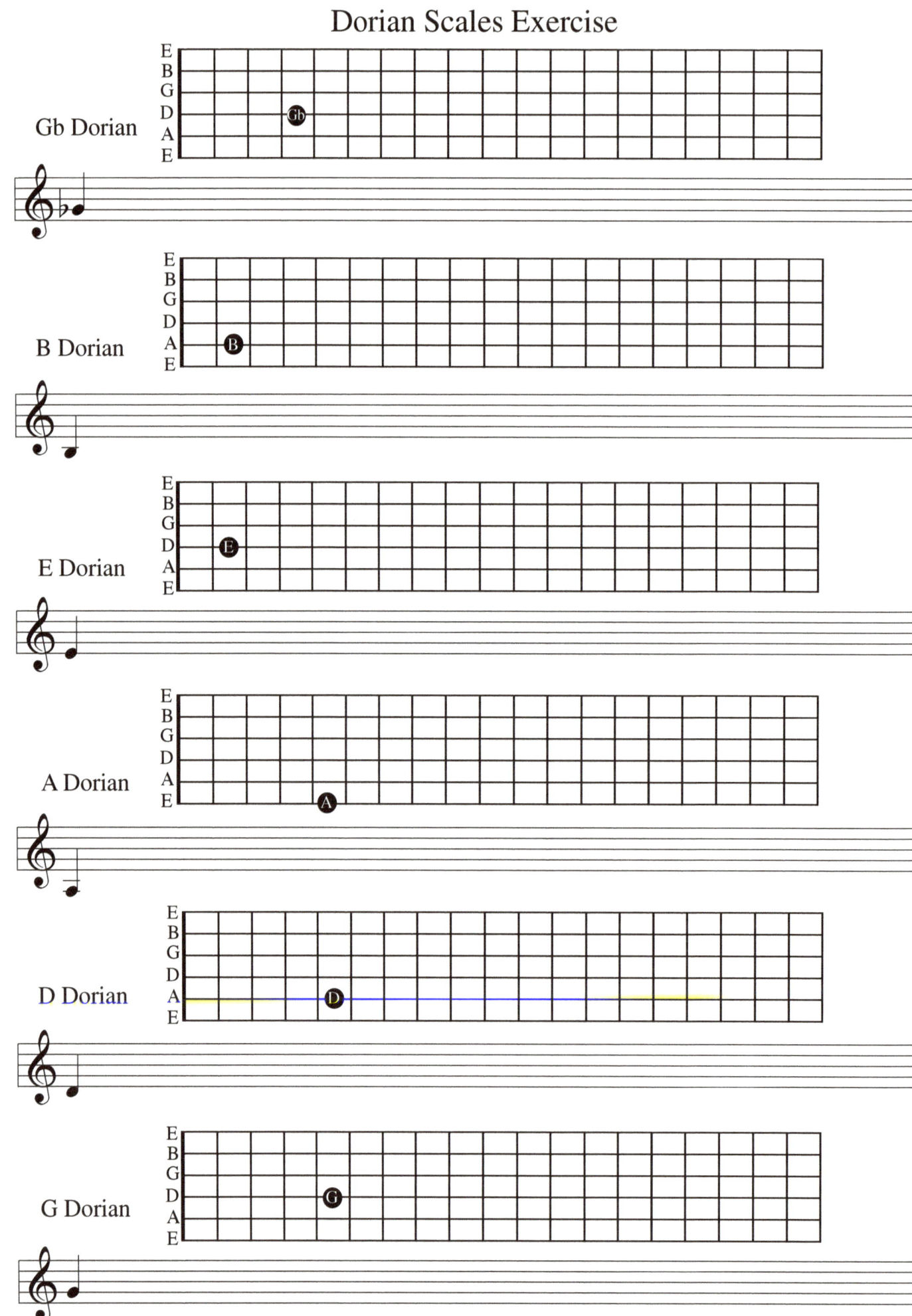

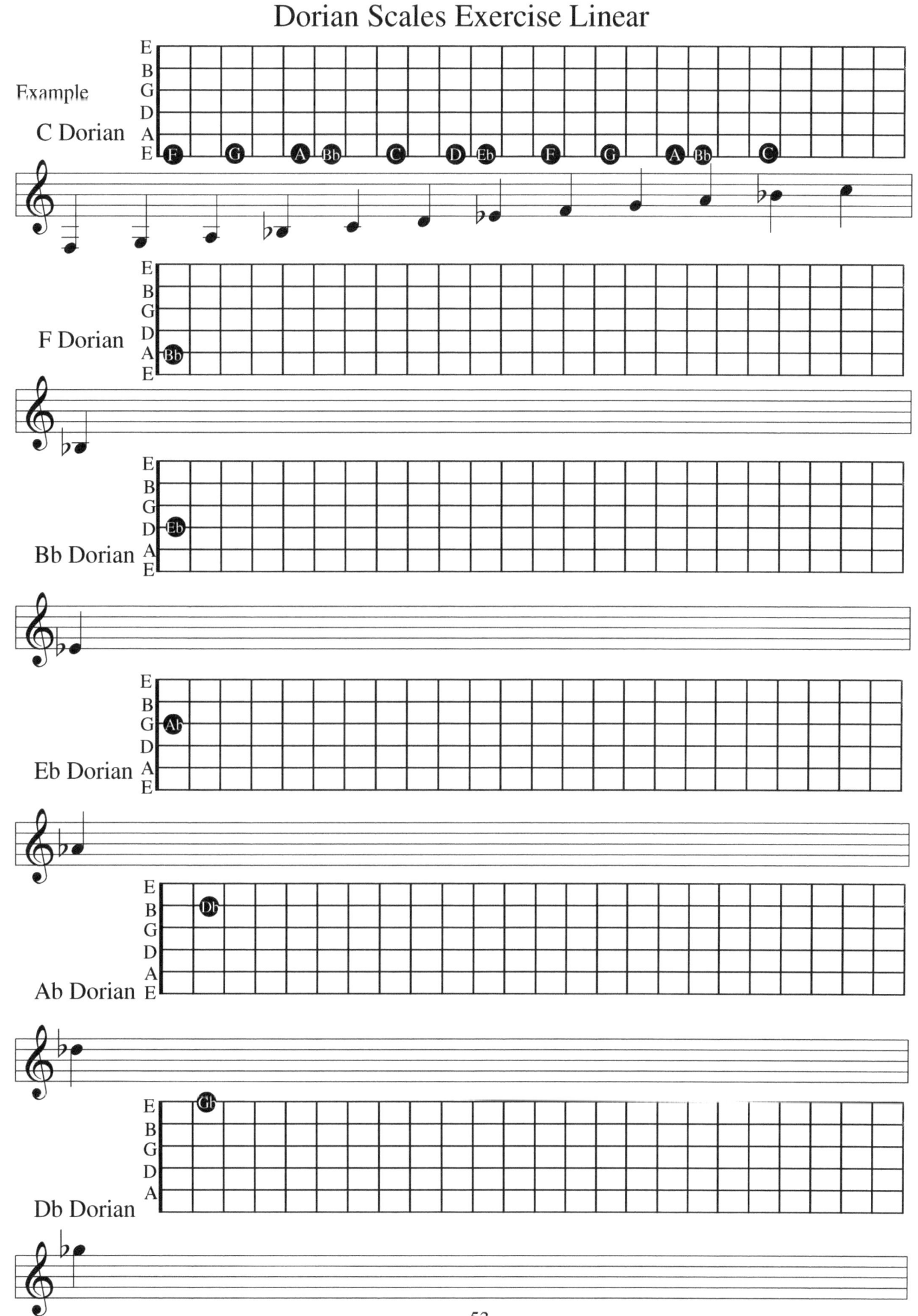

Dorian Scales Exercise Linear

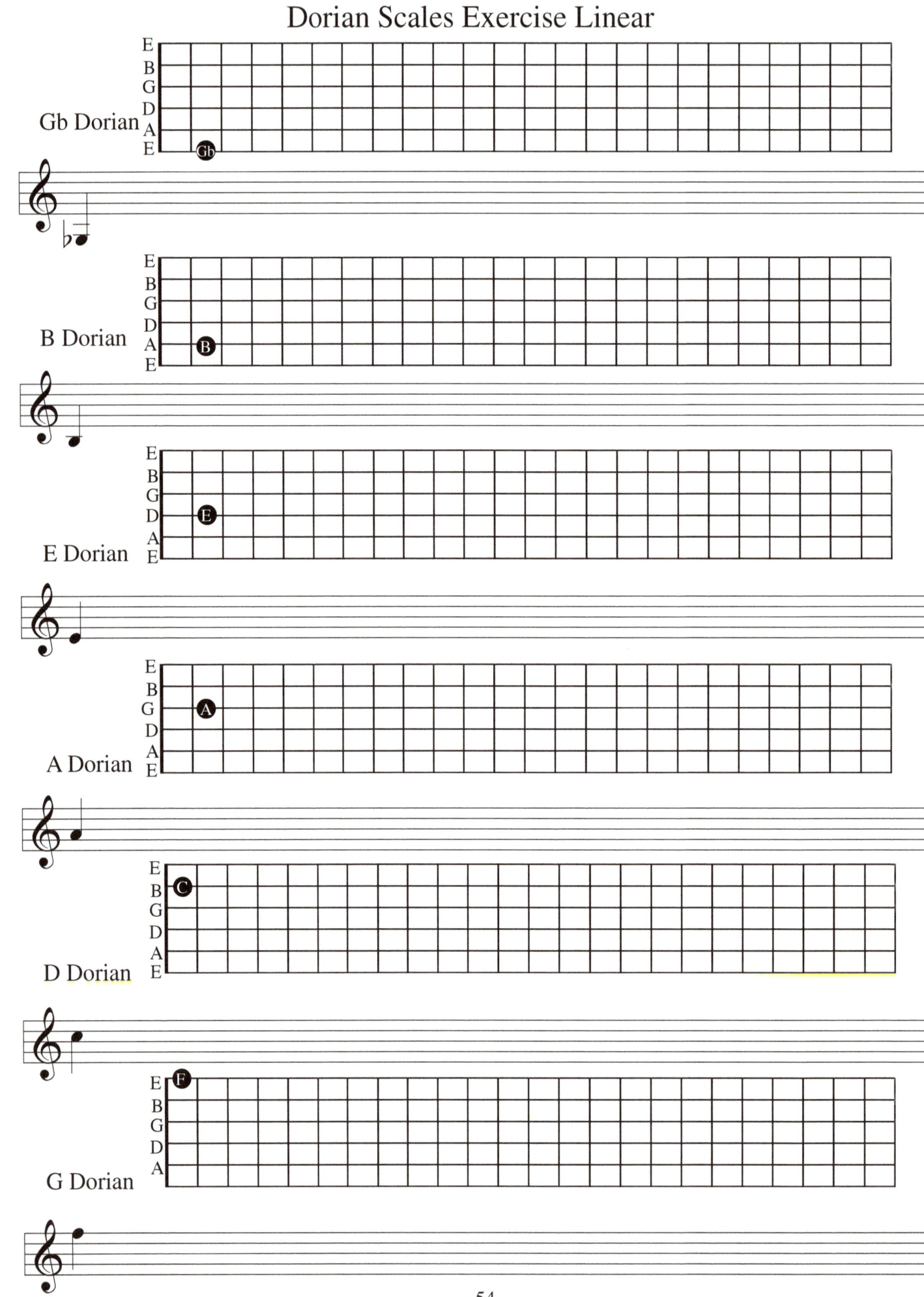

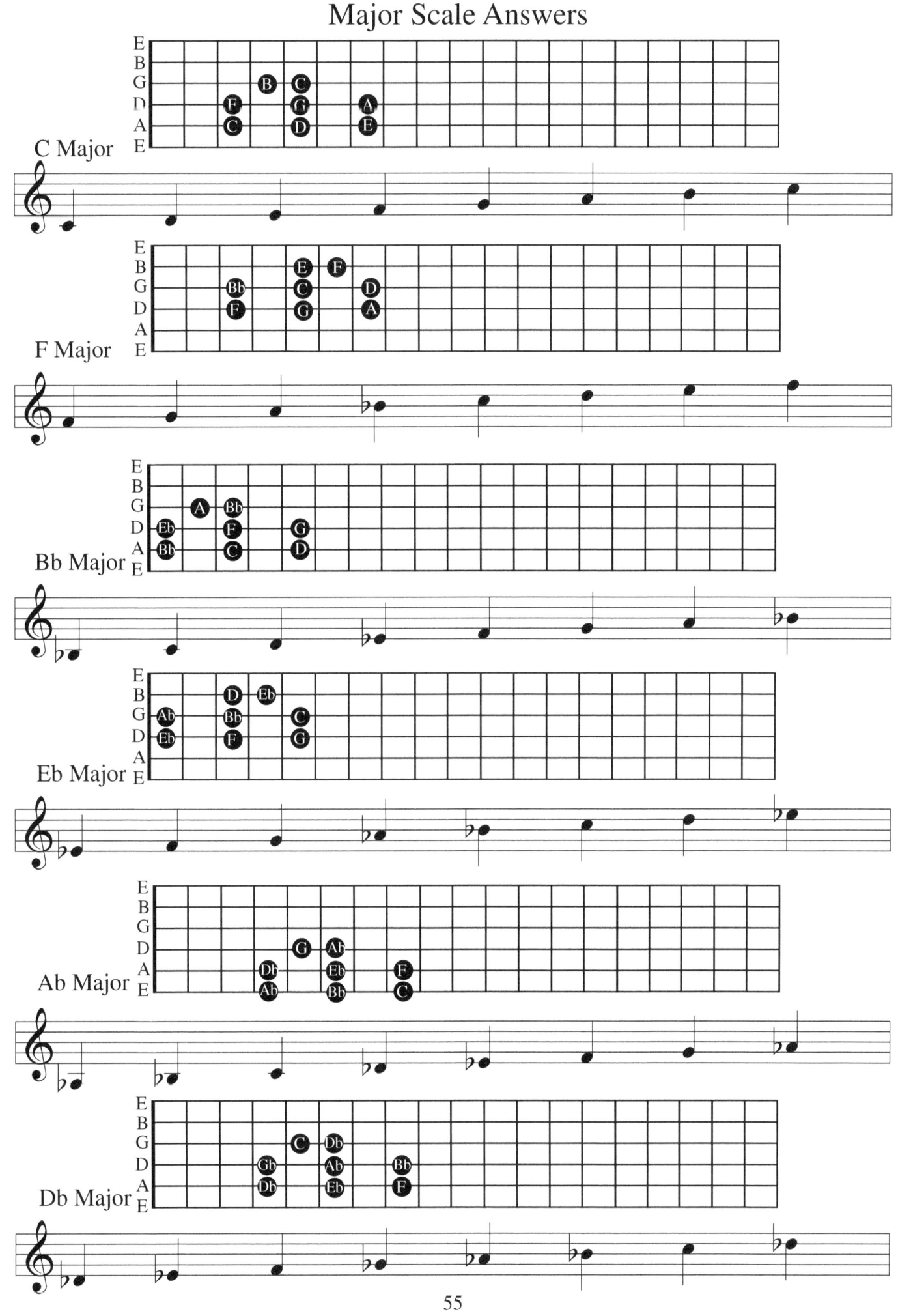

Major Scales Answers

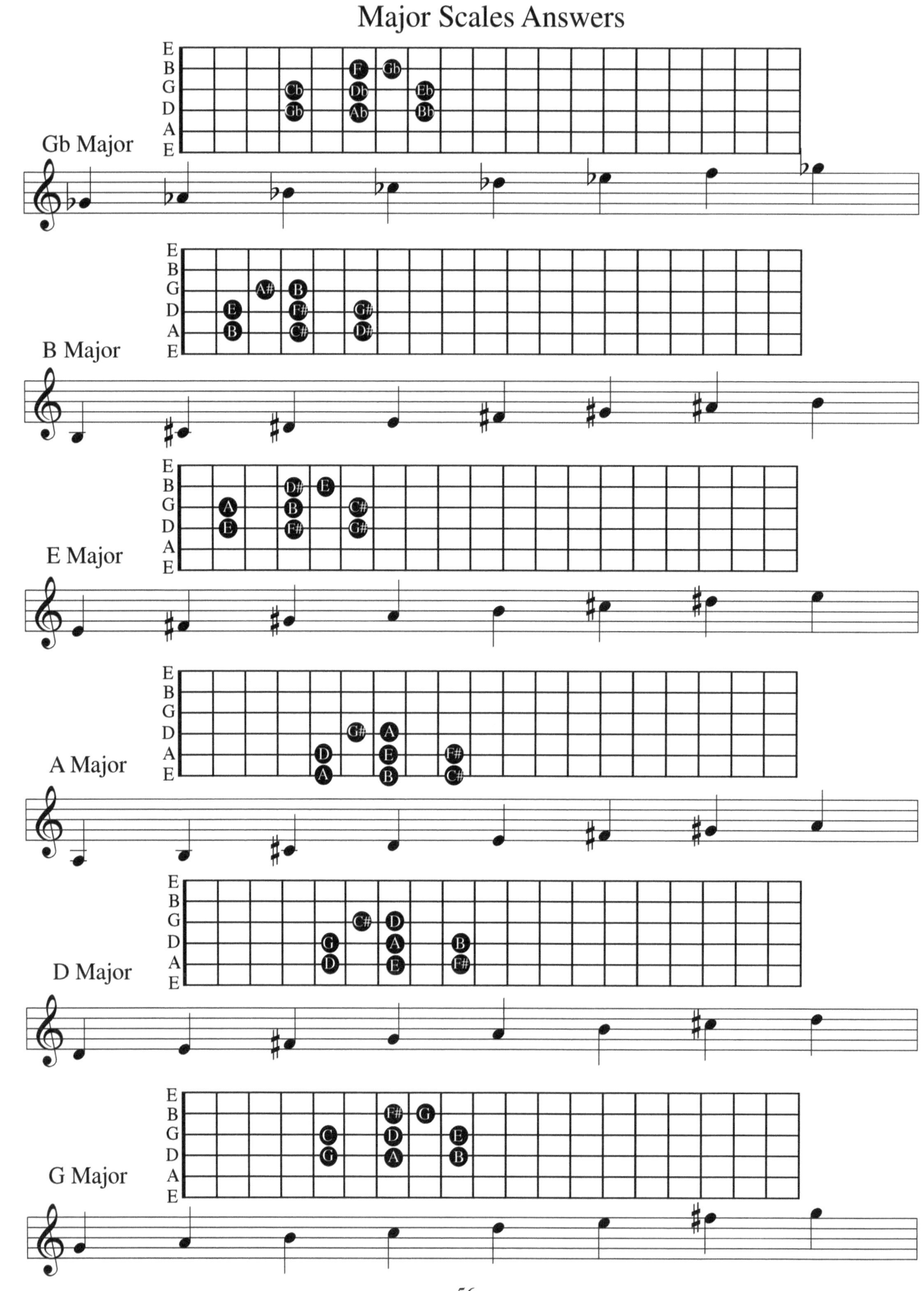

Major Scales Exercise Linear Answers

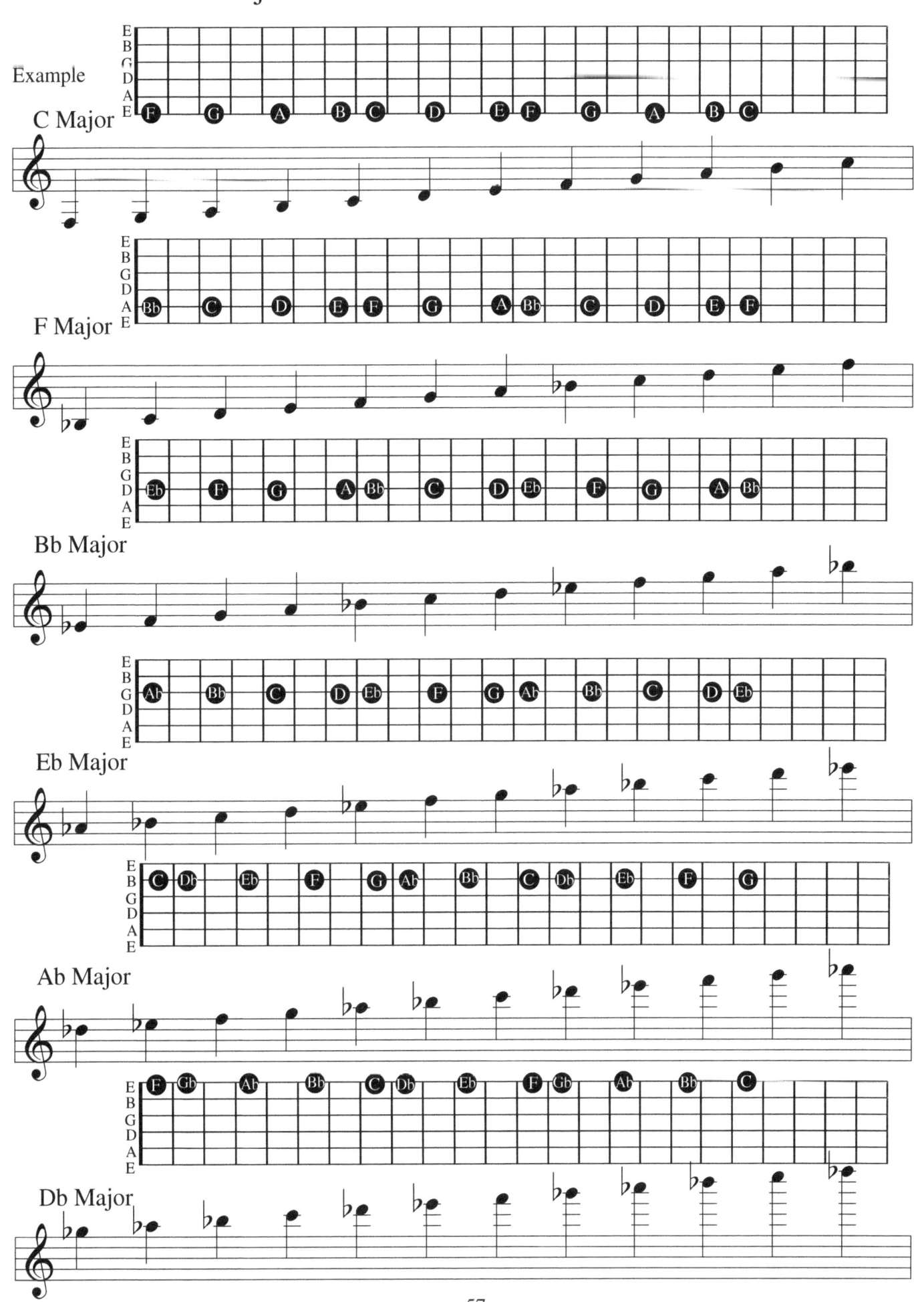

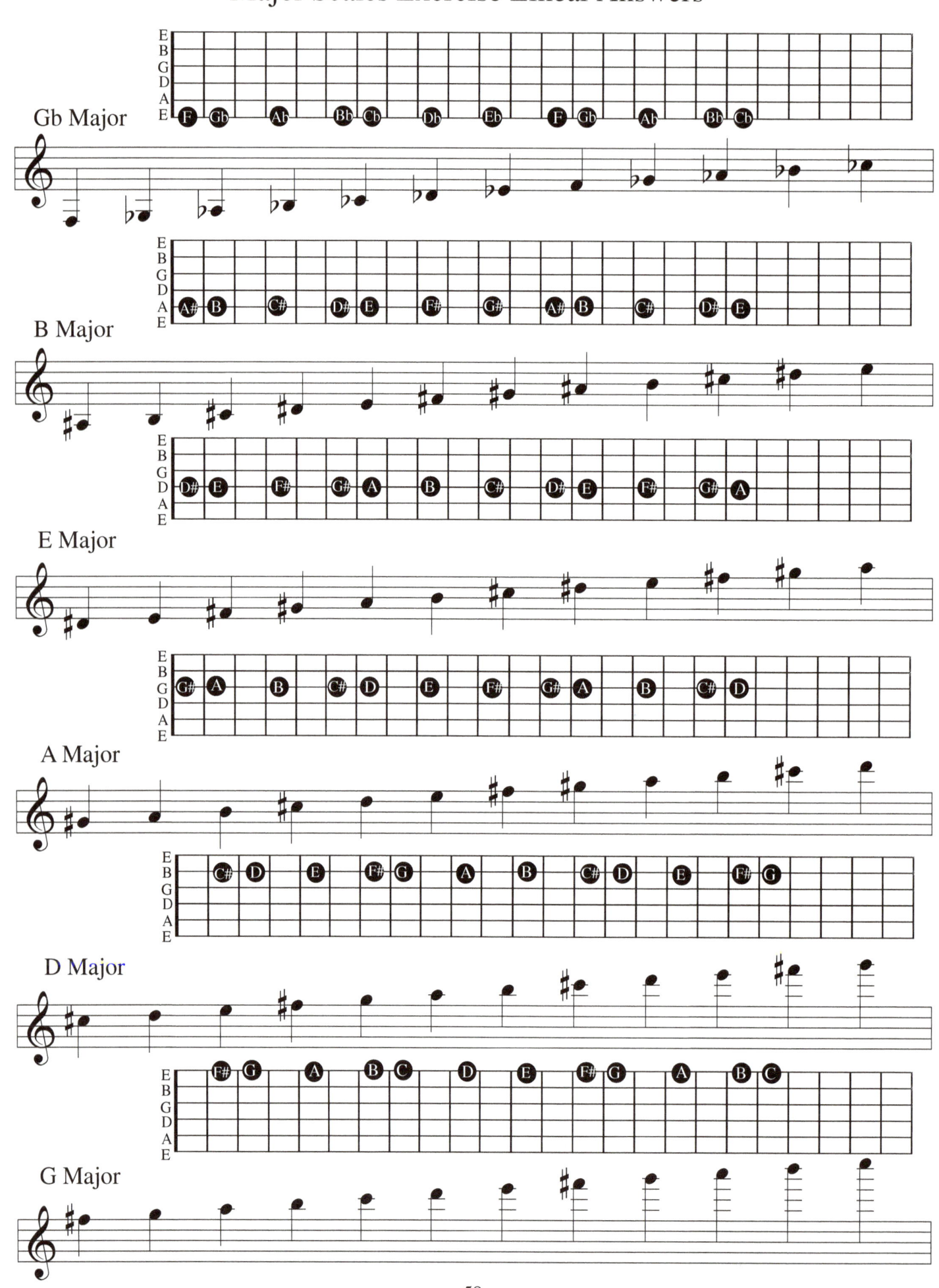

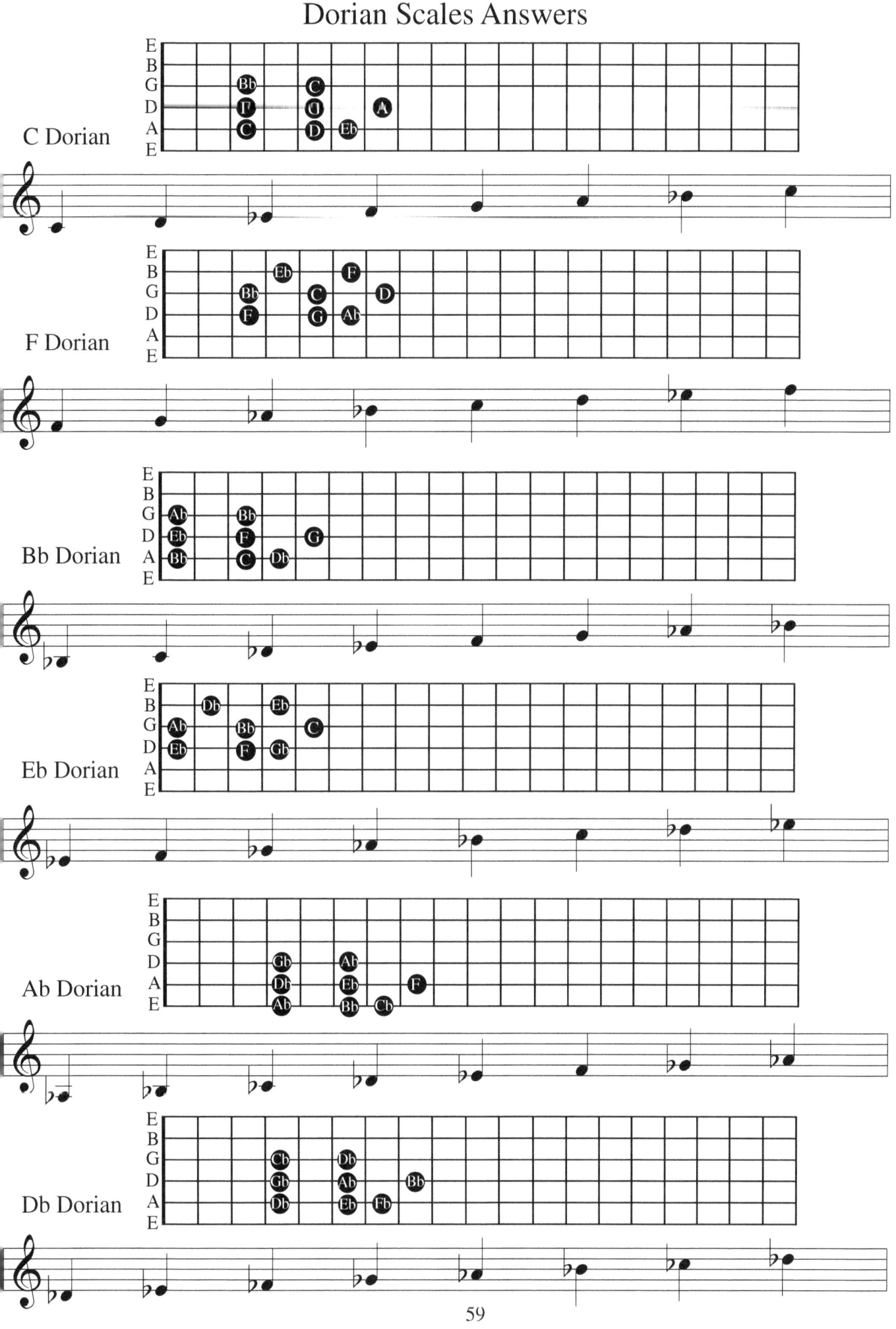

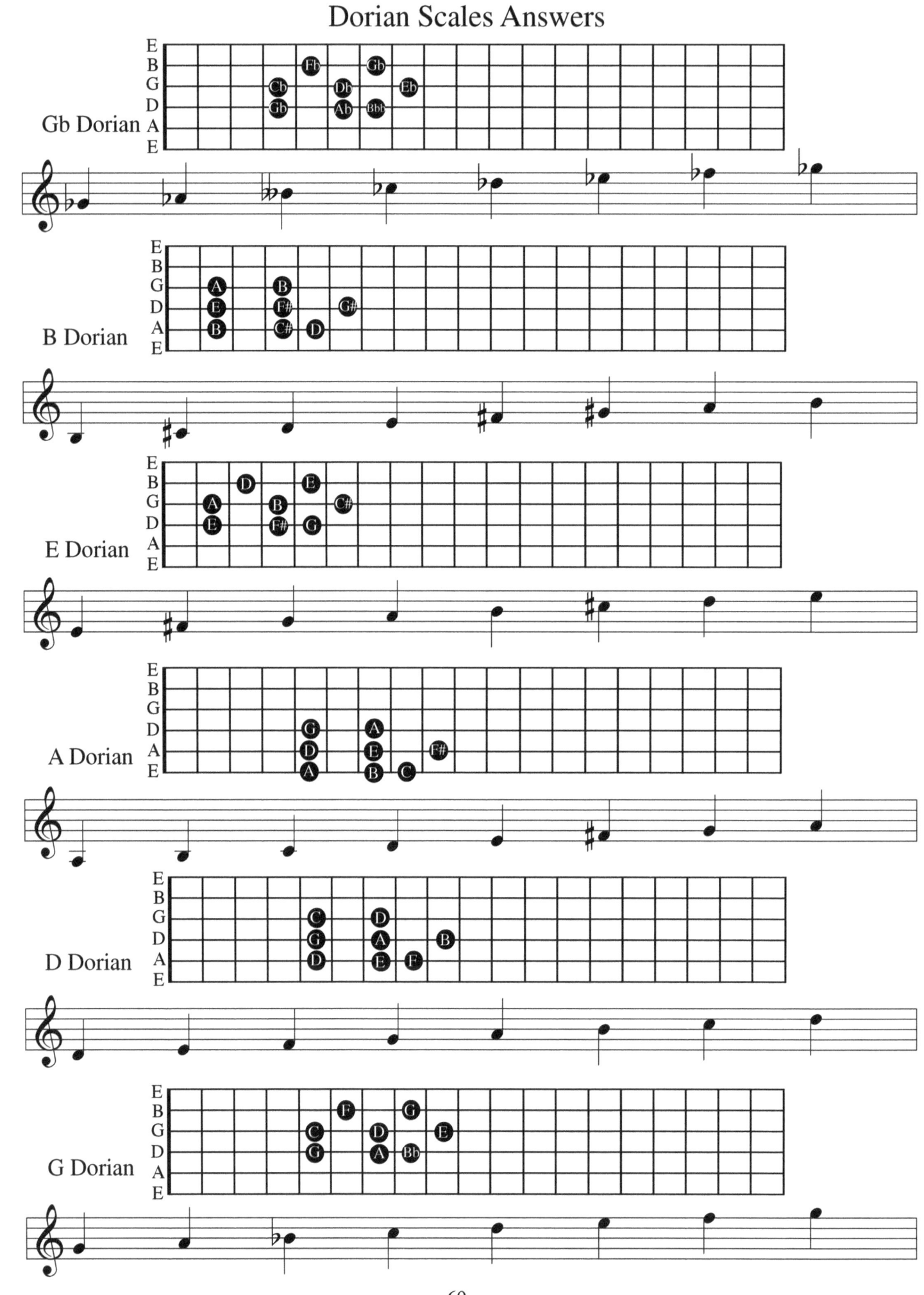

Dorian Scales Exercise Linear Answers

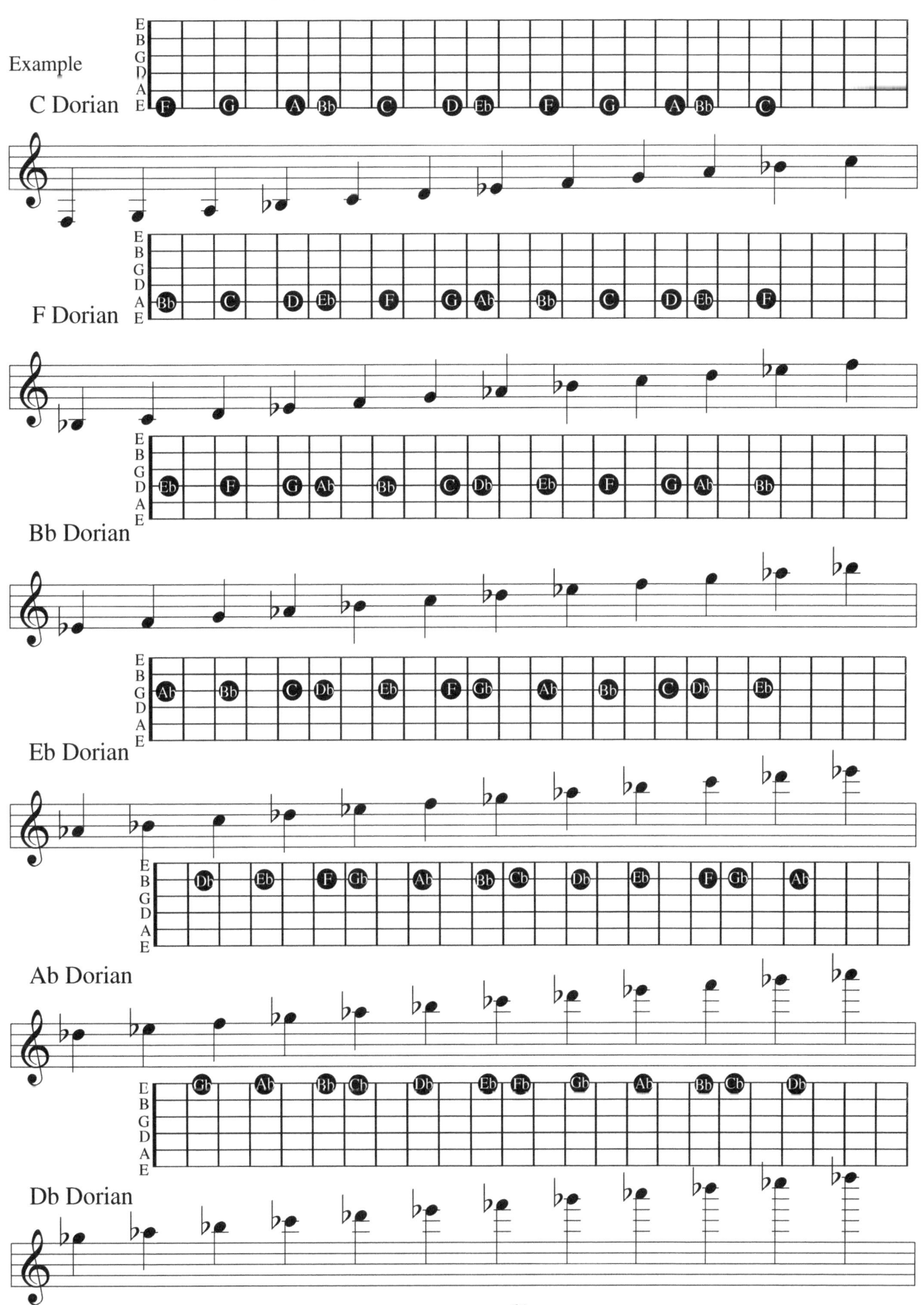

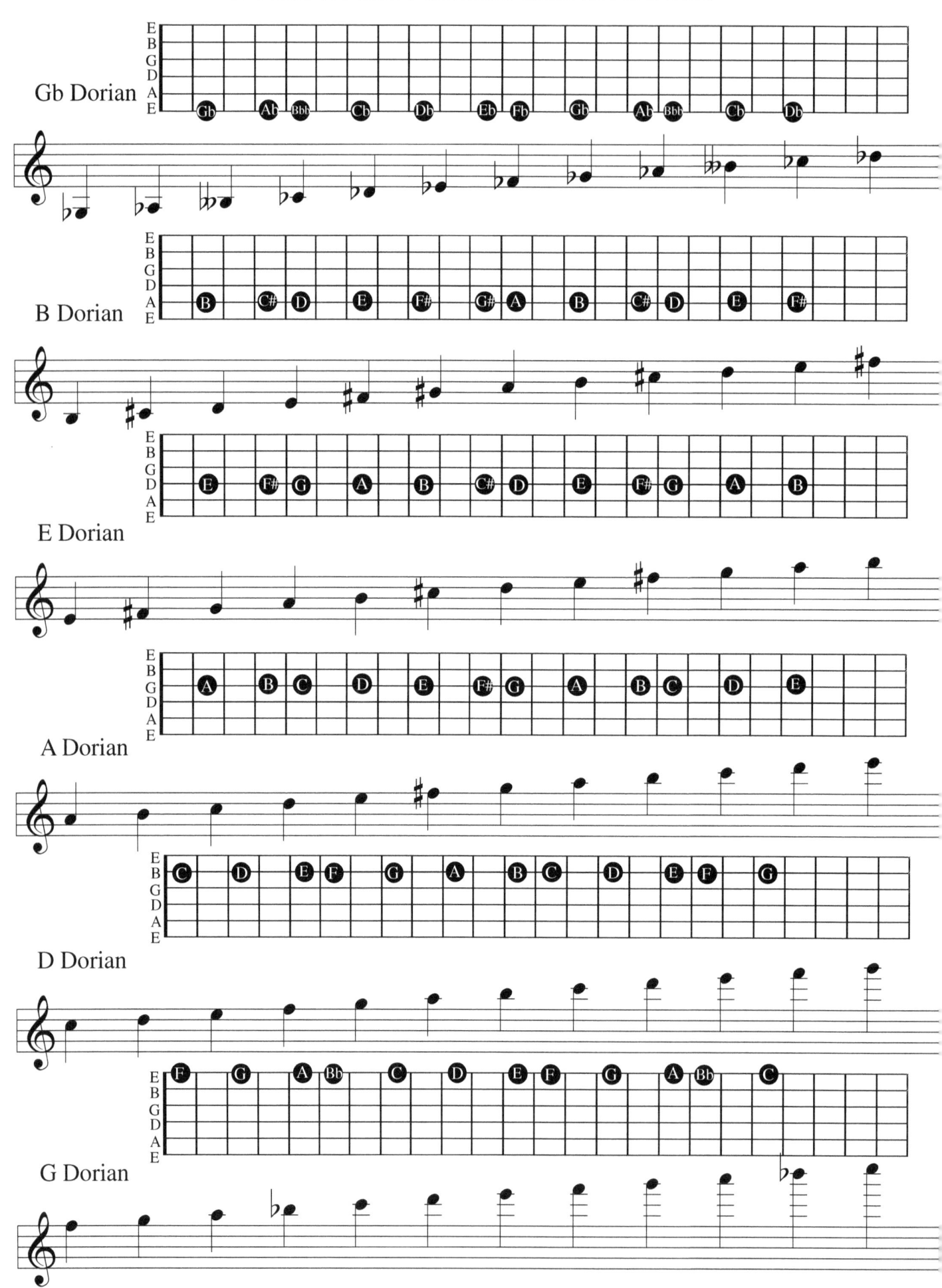

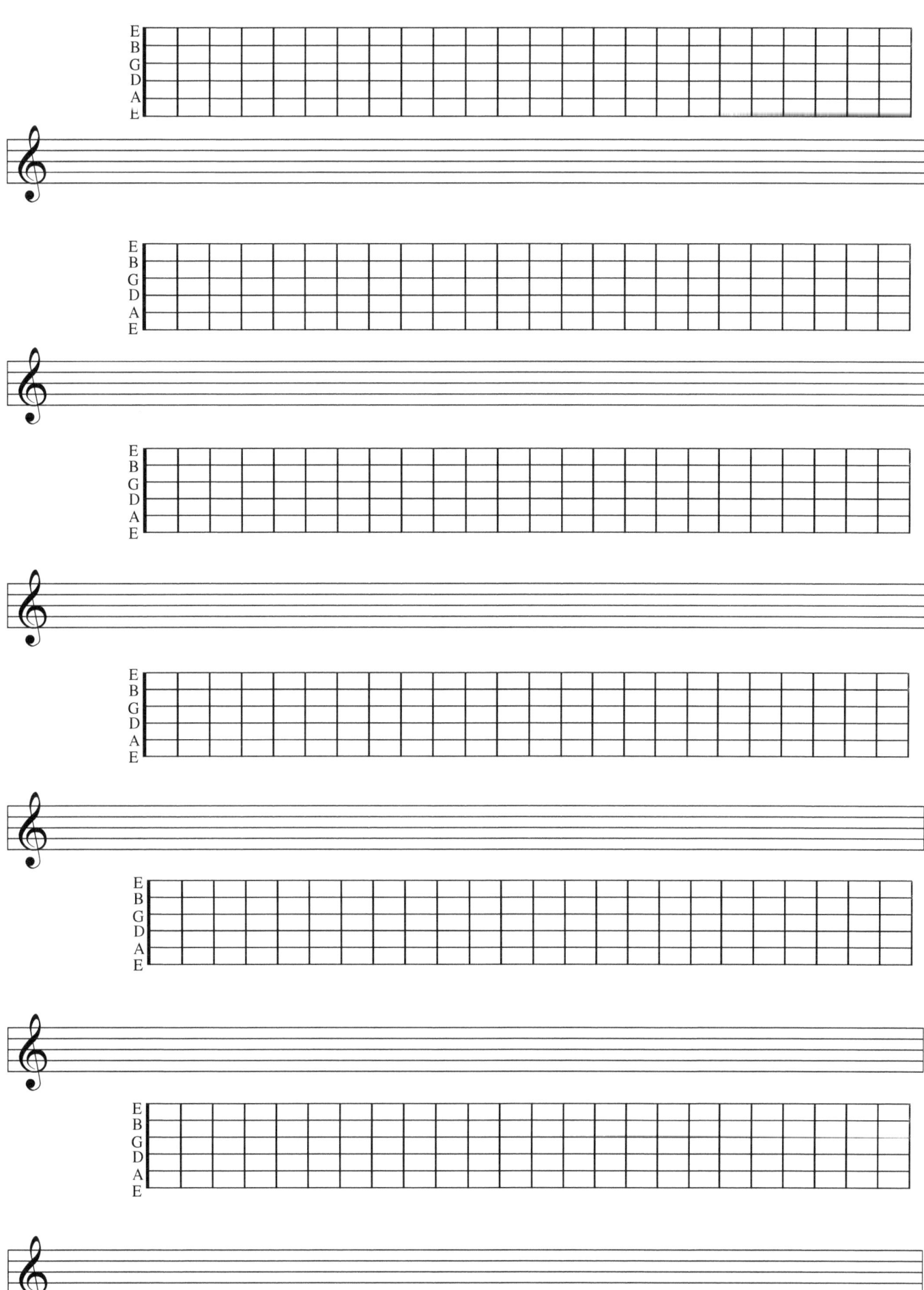

Practice Sheet for Scales from Theory Workbook for Guitar Volume #2 By Bruce Arnold
© 1999 Muse Eek Publishing Company
All Rights Reserved

Fingering for Scales

This portion of the book presents five of the most commonly used scales and how to finger them on the guitar fretboard. Each scale should be learned in every key and also should be applied to chord progressions. Audio files containing chord progressions to help in applying these scales can be found on the muse-eek.com website.

Pages 65-66 contain the fingering for the major and dorian scales. Each scale is presented in all the possible positions it can be played on the guitar fretboard. By learning every scale starting from every degree you will have a working knowledge of the scale anywhere on the fretboard. This is important in order to help access a scale no matter where you are on the guitar neck. As previously mentioned it is important to learn the notes or degrees rather than the fingering patterns. If you are new to these scales I recommend saying the names of each note out loud until you feel you know each note. I also recommend saying the degrees out loud. For example, if you are playing a C major scale starting from C you would say "one" for C, "two" for D, "three" for E, etc. You should also learn each scale in all keys as recommended at the bottom of the page of each scale pattern. Notice in the upper left hand corner a listing of what chord(s) each scale can be used over.

Proper Technique

Tension is <u>never</u> part of good technique.
You need to keep the fingers of your left hand (the hand fretting the guitar neck) relaxed. In general you should not stretch your fingers out to cover each fret. You should move your hand up or back depending on the direction you are moving. This keeps your hand in a constantly relaxed position. Your fingers should stay as close to the neck as possible; this will greatly improve your accuracy and speed. Your hand should keep a uniform shape as it moves up and down the scale. Your thumb should maintain a position approximately between the index and middle finger. A short video of this technique can be found in the "members section" of the Muse-eek.com website. As an owner of this book you are entitled to use this resource. Just register on the site and get your username and password.

Practice Schedule

I recommend learning a new scale each week. You can either take one scale like the major and learn it in each key, one per week, or you could learn a new mode in one key per week. (C major in week one, C dorian week two etc.) I highly recommend you work with either or both "Music Theory for Guitar Volumes One and Two" as you learn each scale. This will ensure that you are learning the fingering and the theory of each scale.

More Scale Resources

The "Music Workshop" located at www.arnoldjazz.com contain 19 scales that can be downloaded for free to further develop your scale vocabulary. This site also contains Chords, Arpeggios, Sweeps, Music Theory and other important practice tools.

C Major Scale (all 7 positions on guitar)

This C major scale should be learned by thinking the notes i.e. C,D,E... or by thinking the degrees C=1, D=2, etc., Do not just memorize a fingering pattern. After you have mastered the C scale in every position. You should learn these scale forms in all keys. Use Cycle 5 to move through the keys i.e. C then F, Bb, Eb, Ab, Db, Gb, B, E, A, D, G. Remember always think the notes or the degrees. Good Luck!

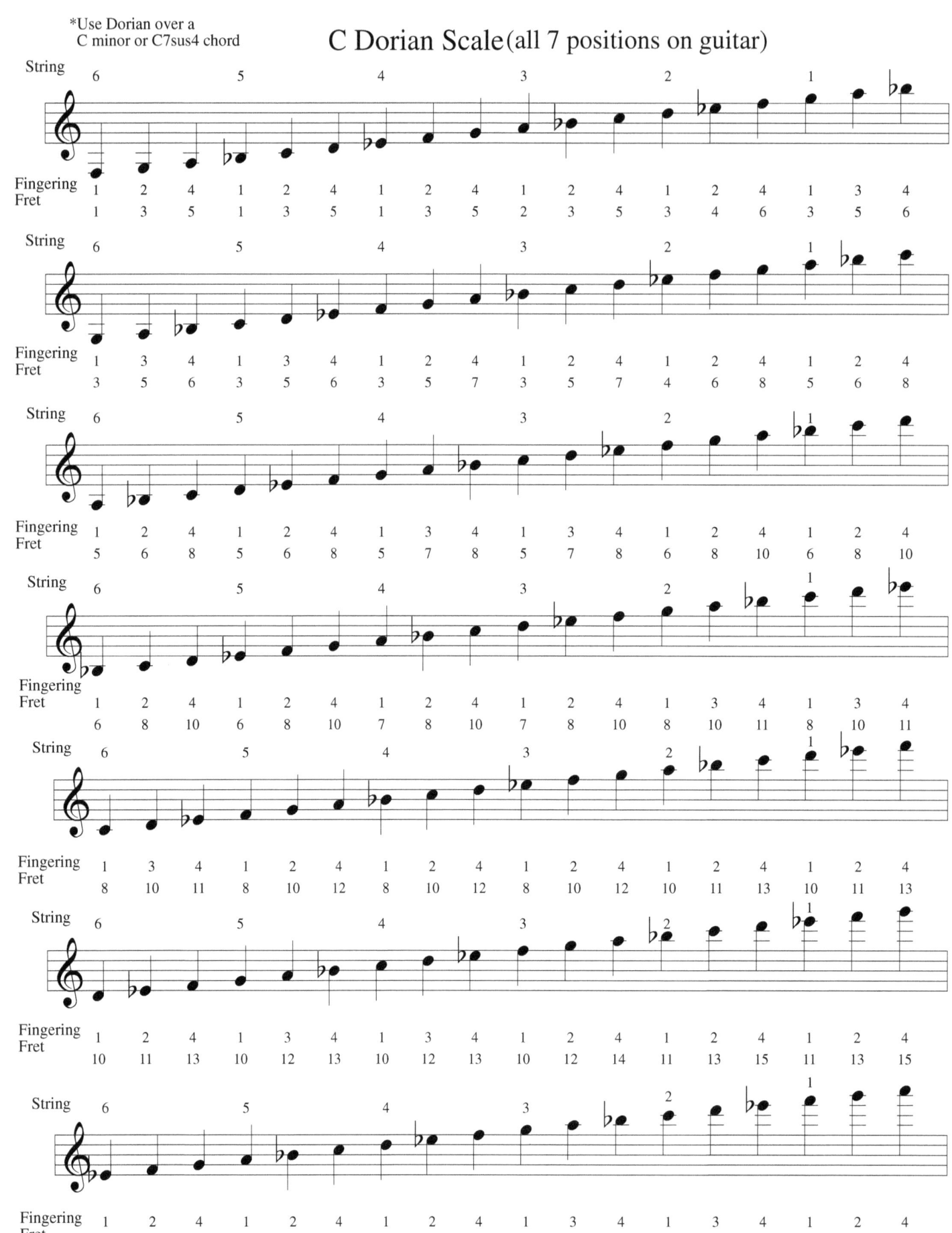

Pentatonic Scales

The "Pentatonic" is a five note scale. There are 38 possible pentatonic scales times 5 modes so pentatonics can be a rich resource for improvisation and composition. The two most commonly used are referred to as the "major" and "minor" pentatonic scales.

Page 68 presents the "major" pentatonic scale with its 5 modes or possible places to play on the guitar fretboard. You should learn each position of the scale keeping in mind the proper technique discussed on page 64. With the major and minor pentatonic scales, stylistic considerations play an important part in the way a scale sounds. For guitarists, embellishments such as bends, slides, hammer-ons and pull-offs are used to give the pentatonic scale the characteristic sound so commonly found in blues, rock, R and B, country and other contemporary idioms. Along with learning the scales it is important to transcribe solos from other players to learn exactly how the pentatonic scale can be applied.

In general a major pentatonic is played over a major, dominant or sus4 chord. The minor pentatonic is played over a dominant, sus4 or minor chord. You will also hear players using a minor pentatonic over a major chord. The pentatonic scale is also used over entire chord progressions. Usually these chord progressions are all diatonic to a key center. You will need to know what the diatonic chords are for a specific key to apply this technique. (See page 29 for explanation of diatonic chords of a key-mode).

Many students get confused about the difference between the major pentatonic and the minor pentatonic because they are both modes of the same scale. For instance, a C major pentatonic scale (C,D,E,G,A) and an A minor pentatonic scale (A,C,D,E,G) have the same notes. **It is important to realize that a scale is given its name based on the key you hear it in, not the notes contained in the scale.** Therefore if you are playing in the key of A minor the notes A,C,D,E,G would be called an A minor pentatonic. If you are playing in the key of C major the notes C,D,E,G,A would be called a C major pentatonic. You can use this connection between these two scales/keys as a way to apply pentatonic melodies you know in A minor to the key of C, and visa versa.

Learn both pentatonic scales in all keys. As you work through each key remember to think the notes or degrees and don't just memorize the pattern. Use the audio files found on the Muse-eek website to help you learn to improvise with the scale, or use your favorite tunes. The nice thing about pentatonic scales is that they work over most chord progressions.

C (Major) Pentatonic Scale
5 positions on guitar

C (Minor) Pentatonic Scale
5 positions on guitar

Blues Scale

The blues scale is one of the most commonly used scales in contemporary music. One of the major reasons for this is a blues scale is based by key not by chord. Therefore by just finding the key center for any progression you can use the related blues scale for the entire progression.

As with the pentatonic scales stylistic considerations play an important part in the way a blues scale sounds. For guitarists, embellishments such as bends, slides, hammer-ons and pull-offs are used to give the blues scale its characteristic sound. Transcribing solos is a good way to learn these embellishments. I suggest you spend most of your time transcribing solos rather than playing the blues scale up and down the fretboard. It is important to know the note names and know this in all keys, but learning the embellishments used with this scale is really the only way to make it sound idiomatically correct.

Because the blues scale is so commonly used over a blues progression a short explanation of that progression is in order. The blues is typically a 12 bar song form with the IV chord coming on the fifth bar. Examples 1 and 2 show you two types of 12 bar blues progression You will find that there are many different ways a blues can be played by substituting different chords but even with these substitutions the IV chord will still be there on the 5th measure. (Use the progressions found on page 77 and 82 to apply the blues scale).

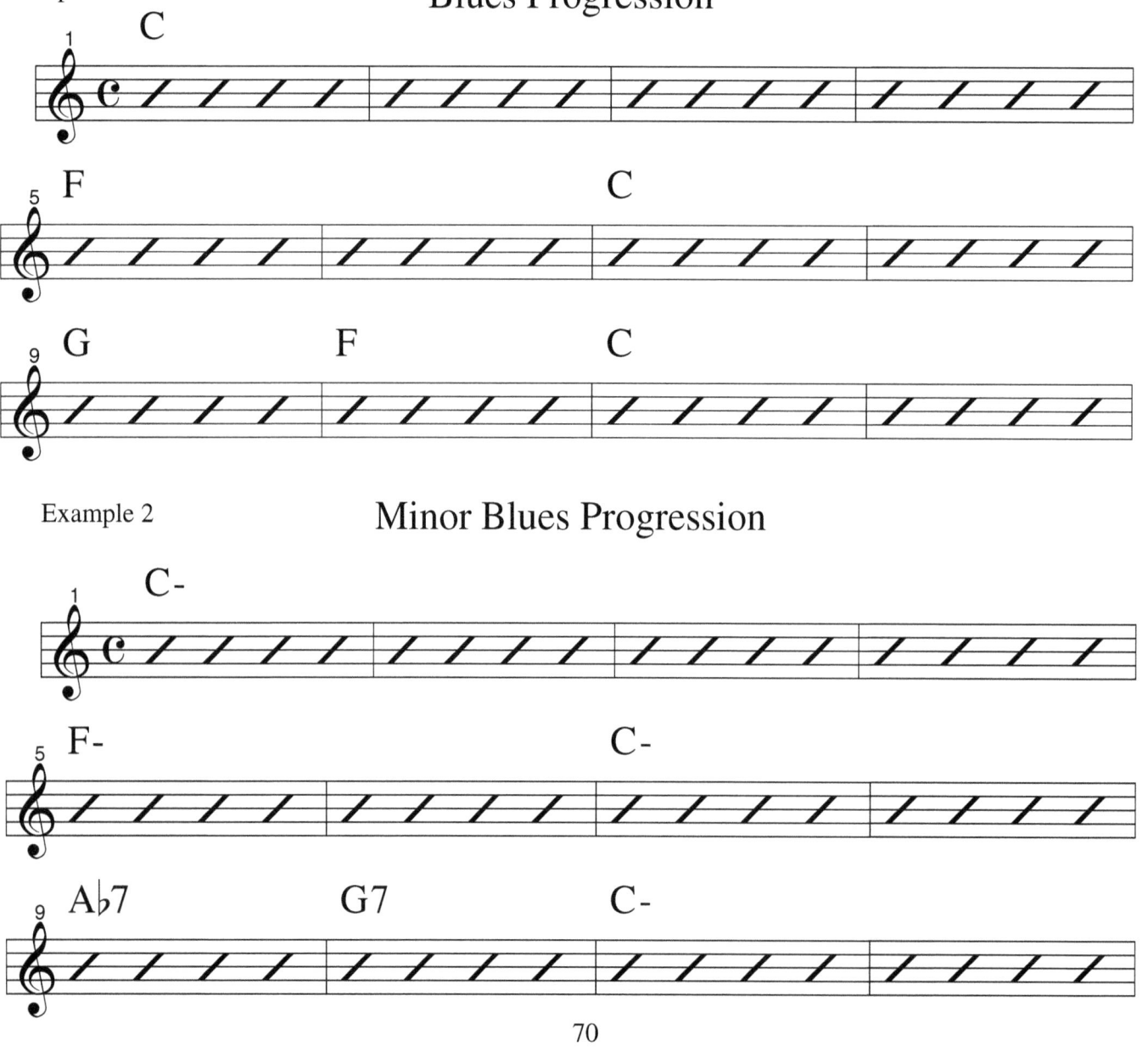

C Blues Scale
(1, b3, 1, #1, 5, b7)

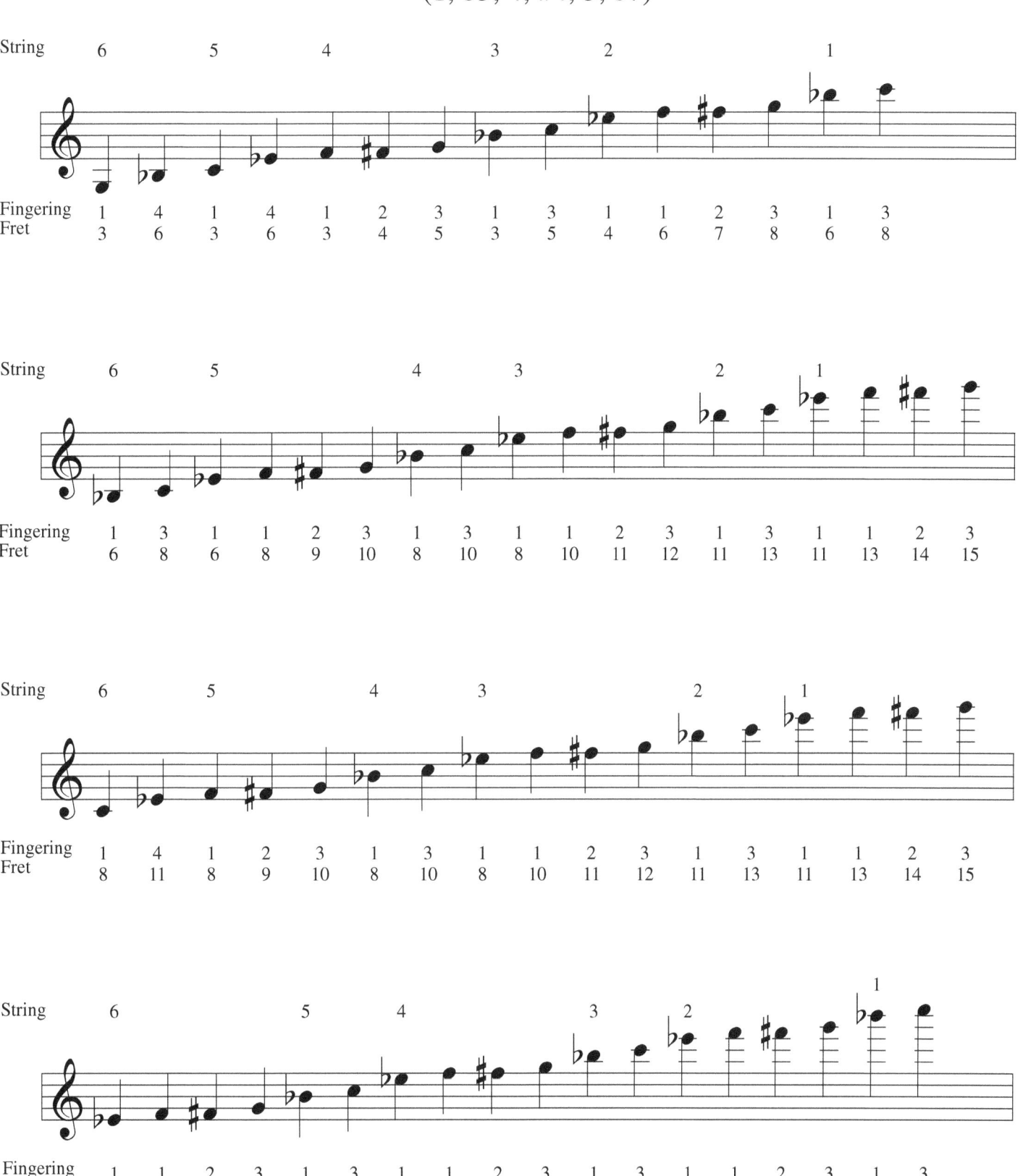

Chords

The chord section of this book is divided up into eight sections.

1. Moveable Chord Forms (p.73)
2. Chord forms used for the C Minor Blues progression (p.74-5)
3. Additional Chord forms used for the F Minor Blues progression (p.76)
4. Chord progression in C Minor and F Minor Blues (p.77)
4. Explanation of upper four string voicings (p.78-9)
5. Chord forms used for the C and F Blues progression (p.80-1)
6. Chord progression in C and F Blues (p.82)
7. Explanation of Bass and Chord Technique (p.83-4)
8. Bass and Chord Technique example (p.85)

A limited number of chord voicings are presented in this book because of space considerations. If you are a beginner you should first work with the moveable chord form found on page 73. More chords can also be found in the "Music Workshop" located at www.arnoldjazz.com. I would also recommend The "Chord Workbook for Guitar Volume One and Two." These two books will give you a well rounded education on chords along with chord progressions to apply each chord voicing. It is also recommend that you work through the "Music Theory Workbook for Guitar Volume One" as you work with chords to reinforce your Theoritical knowledge of each chord. If you are an advanced student move to the progression found on pages 77 or 82. Use the chord reharmonization section found on page 98-99 to help you understand how these progressions were conceived. You may also want to reference the basic blues progressions found on page 70 to compare the reharmonized progression with a basic blues progression. It is highly recommend that you use the "Chord Workbook for Guitar Volume Two" to attain a working knowledge of all upper four string voicings along with working through the 48 chord progressions.

Here's a method for working through this chord section to gain the most benefit from the material presented.

1. Learn all chords form presented in this chord section using the method described on page 73.

2. After learning the chords presented on page 74-6 learn the chord progressions found on page 77. Record these progressions and improvise over each. This is an important way to help you "hear" how these chords sound and to develop a "musical sense" of a 12 bar form.

3. Read about and learn the chord voicing found on page 78-81 using the method described on page 73.

4. Read about and learn chord voicings presented on page 83-4 using the method described on page 73.

5. Learn the chord progression presented on page 85 and apply this technique to other tunes.

Moveable Chord Forms

The chords that follow allow you to learn a chord form and then move it around the neck to get that chord type for every degree of a chromatic scale. All the notated examples of chords should be practiced "cycle 5." Cycle 5 is a way to play all 12 chromatic notes by moving in a pattern of 5ths (or 7 half steps) down from the previous chord. Therefore C moves to F then Bb, Eb, Ab, Db, Gb, B, E, A, D, G. On the guitar this means you would play for example, the first C major chord at the 3rd fret as indicated. Then play the same fingering at the 8th fret on the 5th string and you get F major, then the 1st fret for Bb major, 6 fret for Eb major etc. The example below shows you how to proceed.

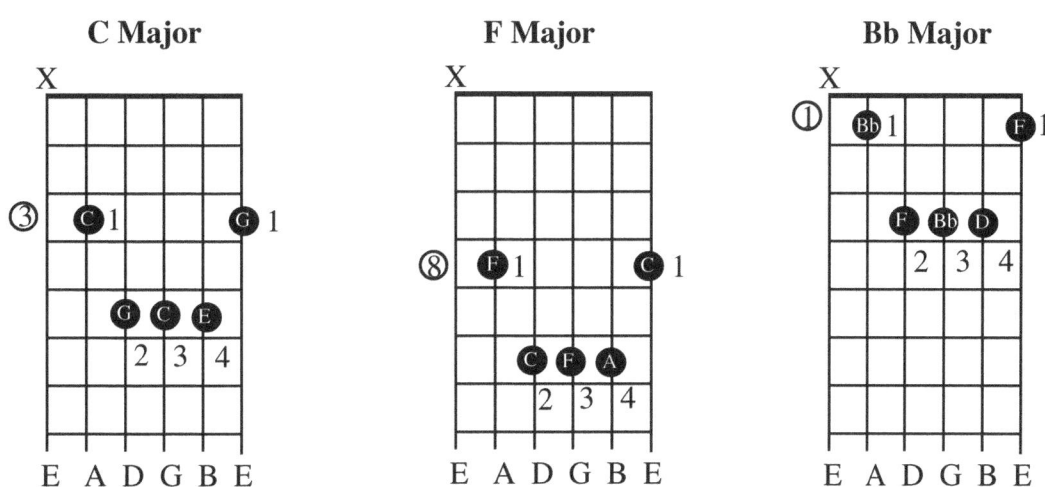

Don't just memorize the position of each of these chords without thinking of what chord you are playing. Memorize, for now, the shape so you can recognize the chord type. Then memorize the bottom of each chord to tell you which chord you are playing as you move through the cycle 5 progression. Remember all examples in this book have the root as the lowest note of each chord voicing so by memorizing the bottom note as you move cycle 5 you will be memorizing the notes on the E and A strings. When you have memorized the notes on the E and A strings you only need to memorize the new chord type as you move through this book.

Cycle 5 is one of the most common chord movements in music. Therefore practicing chords cycle 5 is excellent preparation for playing music.

Cycle 5 Progression or the Circle of Fifths

C, F, Bb, Eb, Ab, Db, Gb, B, E, A, D, G

It is also a good idea to go through the cycle in a couple of ways. For example when you get to Gb think F# instead. Gb and F# are said to be *enharmonic* keys because their pitches are the same on the guitar but their names are different. Refer back to your list of keys to find other enharmonic keys to practice.

Try not to think down a certain number of frets to find the next chord. Memorizing the pitches of each fret will be much better in the long run. All chords contained in this book should be practiced using the cycle 5 movement, and remember when practicing always think what note you are playing rather than memorizing the position.

The next two pages contain the chords used in the C Minor Blues progression found on page 77. First learn all chords presented on these two pages using the method presented on page 73. When applying these chords to the C Minor Blues play the chords on beat one and the "and of two" (see example 1).

Example 1

If you would like to learn other ways/styles to play these chords and chord progressions please see "Comping Styles Volume Two, Funk."

Minor 7th Chords

Chord tones for C-7
1,b3,5,b7

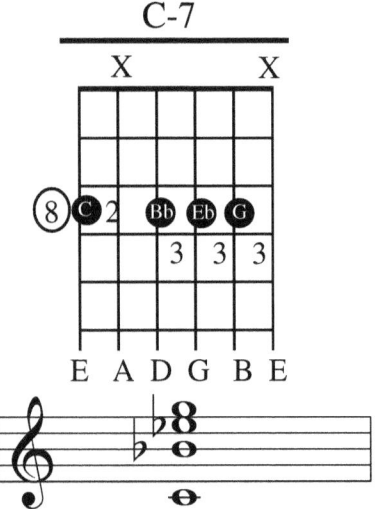

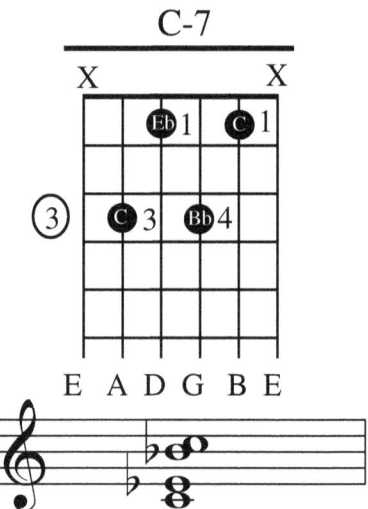

74

Dominant 7#11 Chord

Chord tones for C7#11
1,3,#4,b7

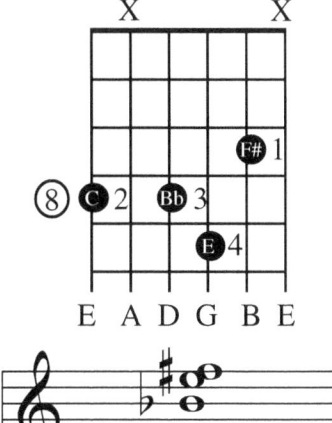

Dominant 7b13 Chord

Chord tones and tensions for C7b13
1,3,b6,b7

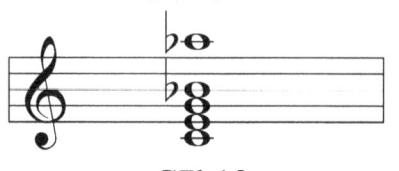

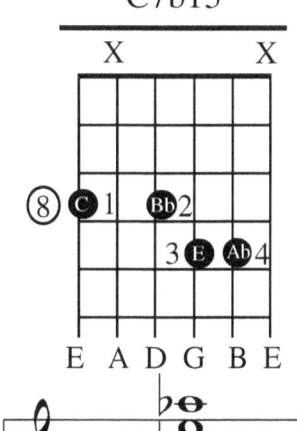

Dominant 7#9 Chord

Chord tones and tensions for C7#9
1,3,5,b7,#9

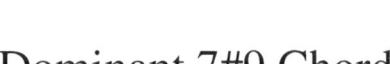

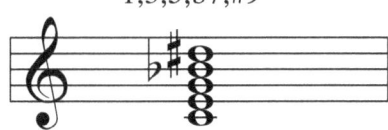

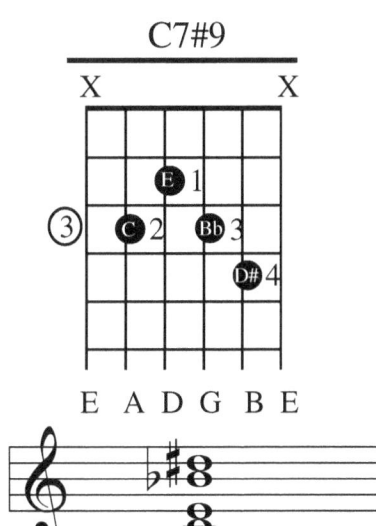

Minor 9th Chords

Possible chord tones and tensions for C-9
1,b3,5,b7,9

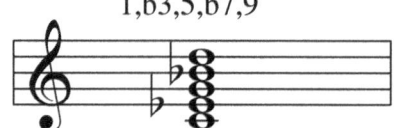

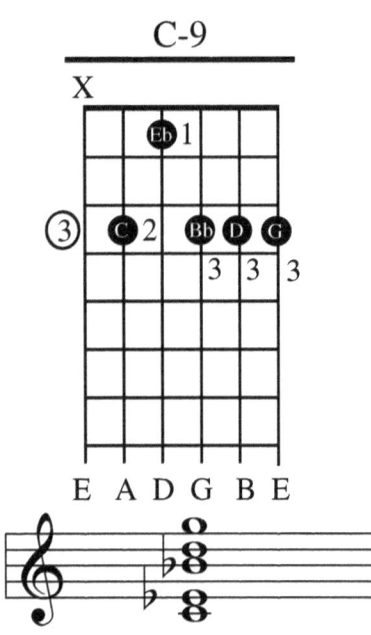

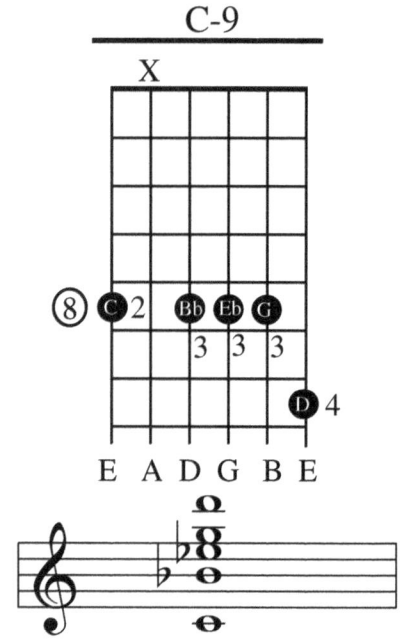

Dominant 7b913 Chords

Possible chord tones and tensions for C7b913
1,3,5,b7,b9,13

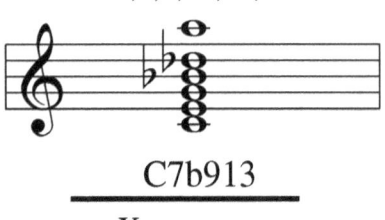

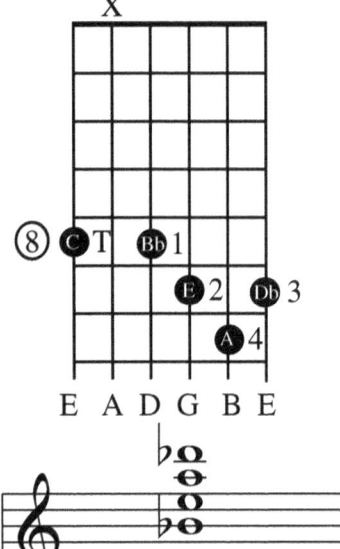

Dominant 9 Chords

Possible chord tones and tensions for C9
1,3,5,b7,9

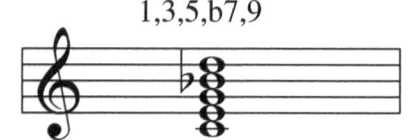

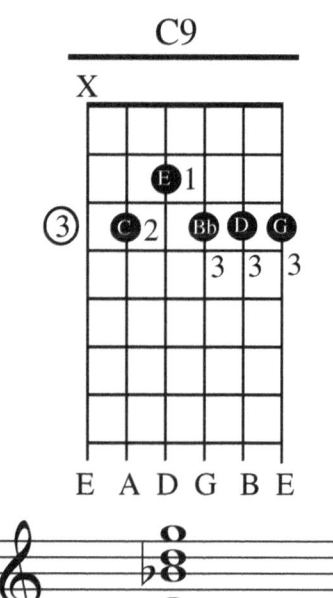

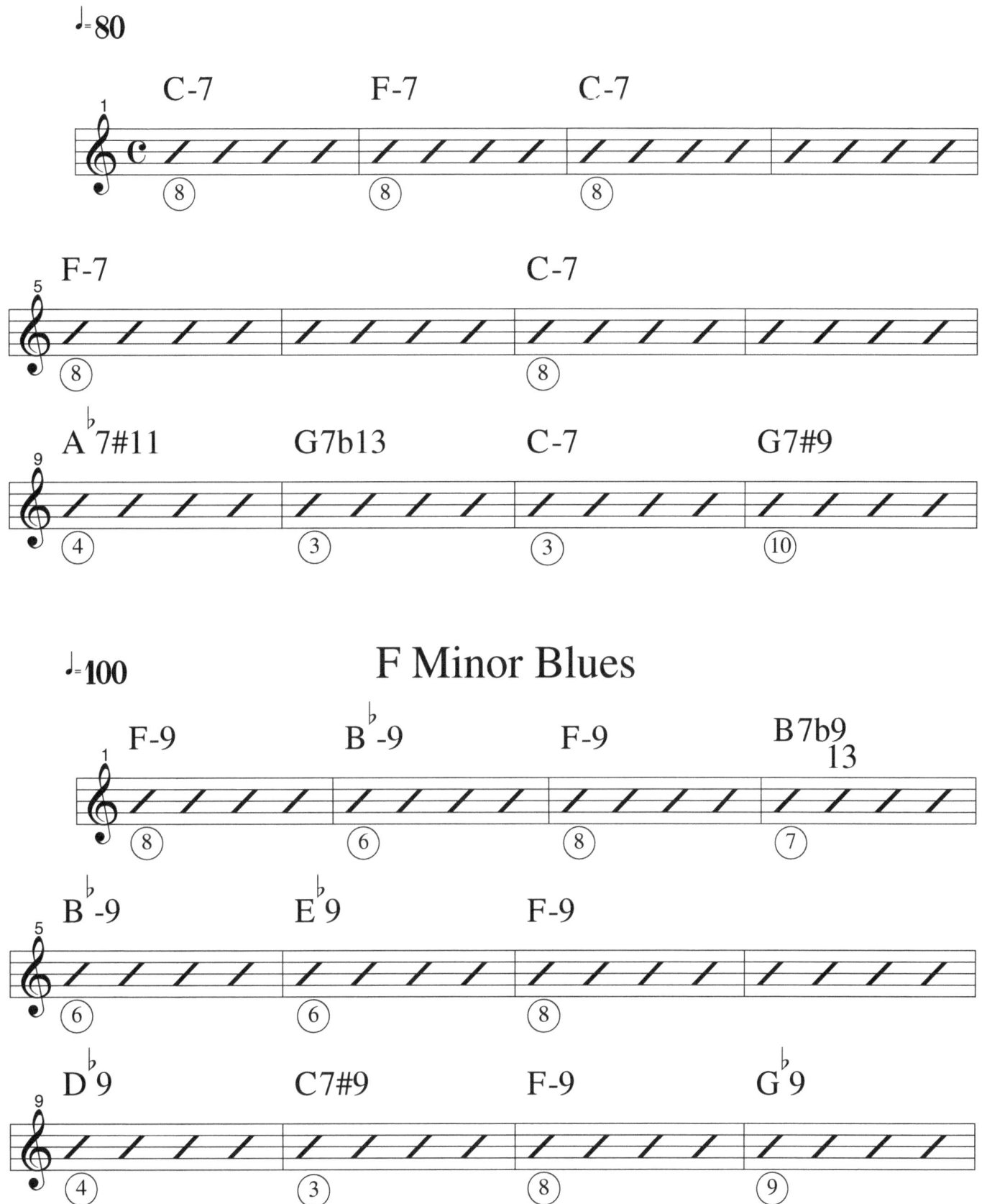

The chords presented so far have always had the root of each chord as the lowest note. This is also called the bass voice. The chord voicing found on the pages 80 and 81 will work with chord voicings that place other notes of the chord in the lowest voice. When a chord places notes other than the root in the lowest voice it is said to be an "inversion". When a chord's lowest note is the root it is said to be in root position.

root position

It is common to call a chord with the 3rd in the bass 1st inversion, with the 5th in the bass 2nd inversion and when the 7th is in the bass 3rd inversion.

If a chord contains tensions it is also possible to place these notes in the bass. The example below shows a CΔ79 with the 9th in the bass.

As more tensions are added to a chord it gets increasingly difficult for a guitarist to play all the notes indicated. Therefore you will find many of the chords presented here have certain notes deleted. The 5th and the root are the most common notes to be left out. It is important to remember that every chord in this book always contains the 3rd and 7th of the chord, with the exception of 7sus4 which has the 4th and the 7th, and the 6th chords which have the 3rd and the 6th.

All chords should first be practiced cycle 5: C,F,Bb,Eb,Db,Gb,B,E,A,D,G. This will help your knowledge of the fingerboard immensely and will also help your hands develop dexterity. It is important to apply these chords in performance situations which is best way to work these sounds into your playing.

Upper Four String Voicings

The upper four string chord voicings presented on the following pages are commonly used in jazz, funk and traditional R&B. For the jazz guitarist these are invaluable chords for accompanying, and because these chords stay out of the bass player's note range they are great for group playing. These voicings are also commonly used in chord melody playing and can be a rich resource for playing intros and solo chord arrangements. As previously mentioned it is also common to find these voicings used in funk music. Listen to early James Brown as a great example of these voicings applied to a funk style. Because the upper four string voicings can be in any inversion the chord possibilities are greatly increased. This on one hand is great because you have a lot of voicings to choose from but on the other hand learning and applying all these voicings can be a daunting task. If you want to thoroughly explore these upper four string voicings I recommend that you work through the "Chord Workbook for Guitar Volume Two."

It is important to learn these voicings in three ways. First learn each voicing so you know what note is in the top of each voicing i.e. the root, 3rd, 5th 7th or possibly a tension. This will help you when you want to use a specific chord type with a specific note in the top voice. Secondly memorize the voicings by what note is in the bottom voice. This will help you when you are moving from one chord to another and will help achieve good voice leading. Third learn where the root is (or assumed root) of each chord. This will help you keep track of what chord type you are using. This is particularly important when chords contain multiple tensions.

I have limited the voicings presented here to easier voicings with limited tensions. By working through the voicings presented in the "Chord Workbook for Guitar Volume Two" in combination with the theory presented on page 98-9 you will have a lifetime of possibilities to enrich your playing.

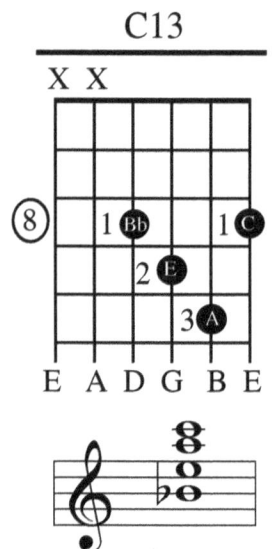
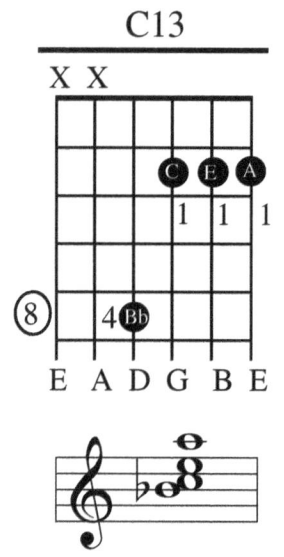
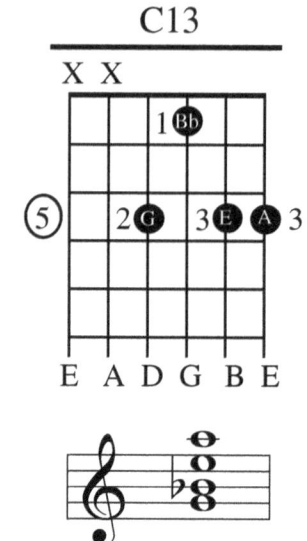
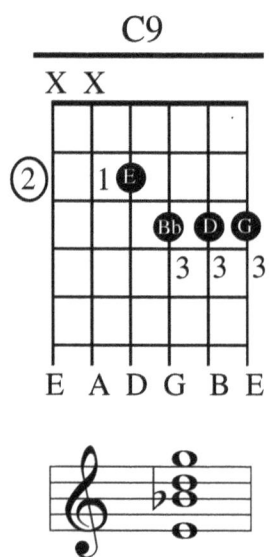
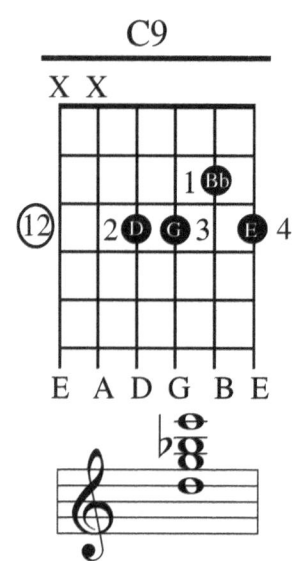
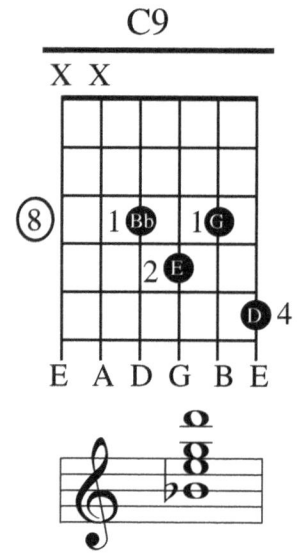
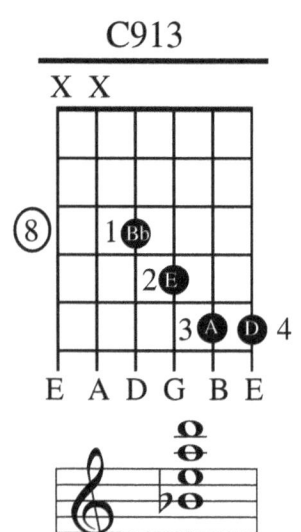
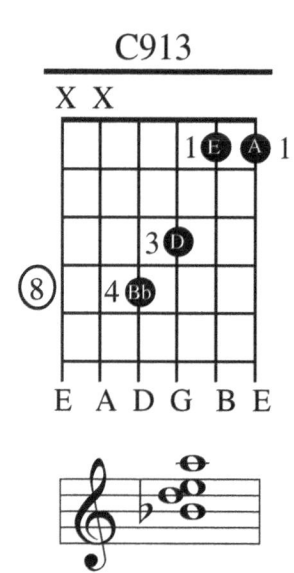
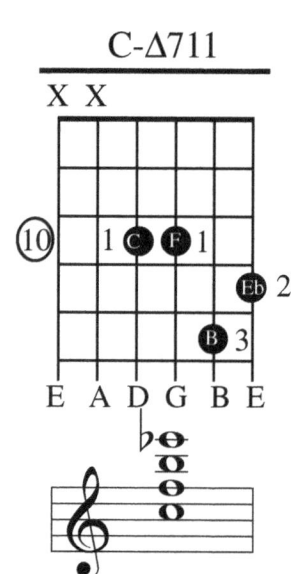

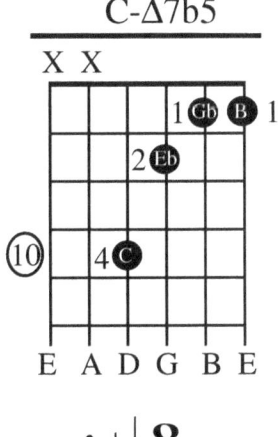
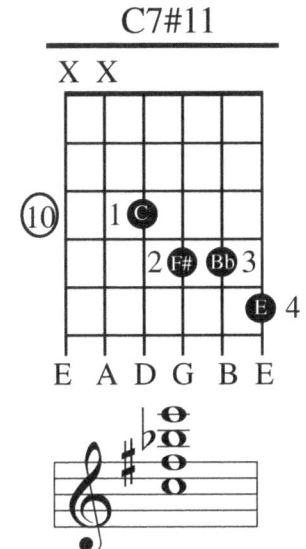
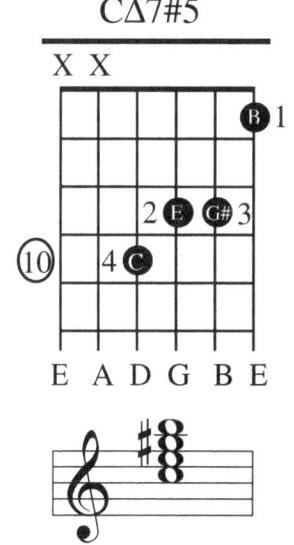
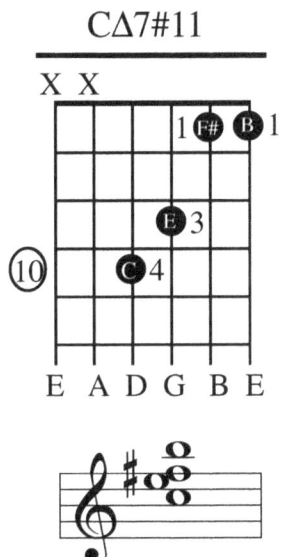
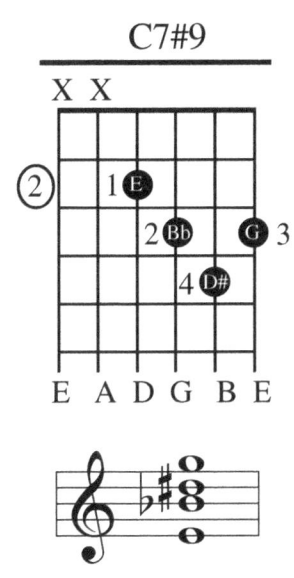
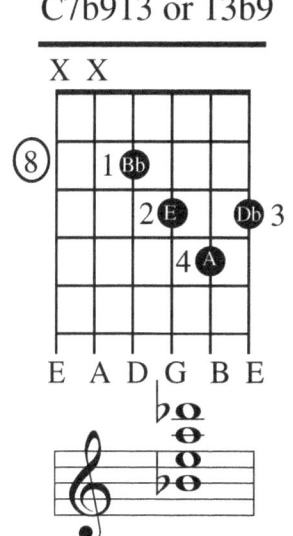

12 Bar Blues in C Major

12 Bar Blues in C Major

Reharmonized

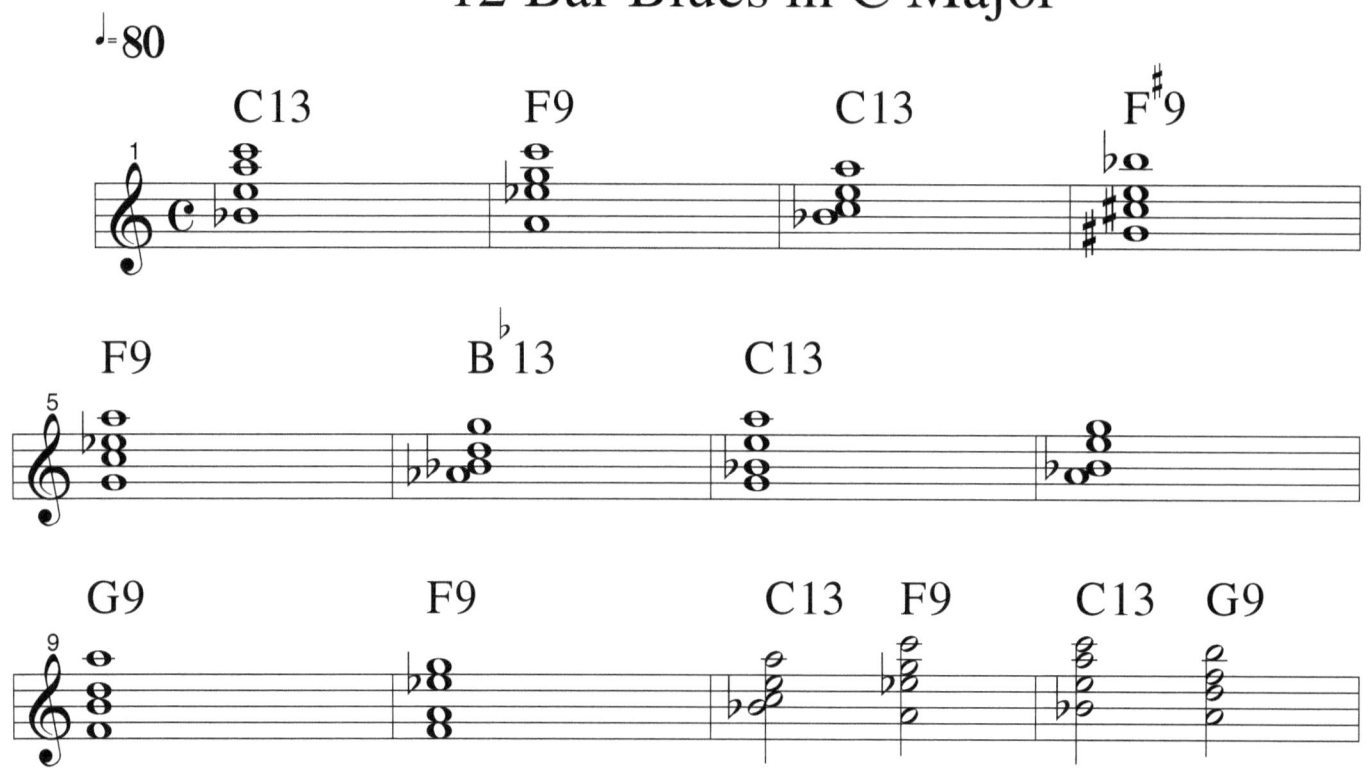

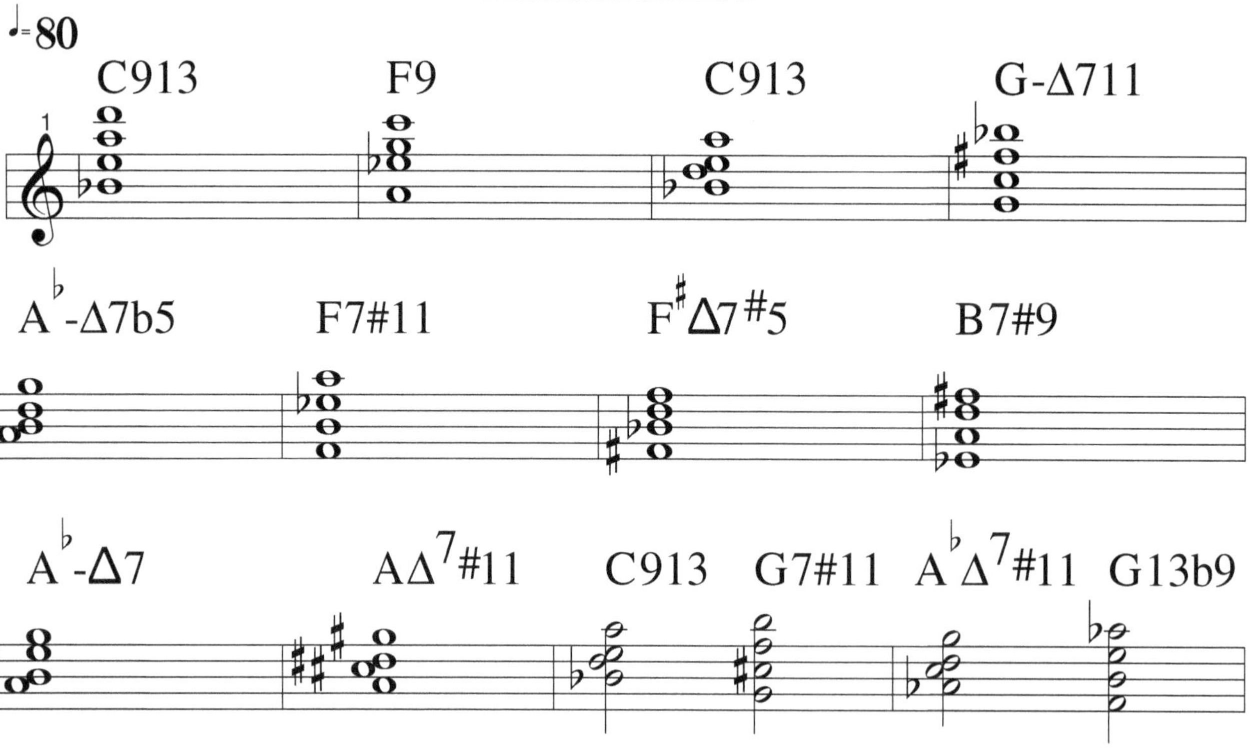

Bass and Chords

The Bass and Chord technique is an interesting way to create the feeling of a whole rhythm section using just a guitar. This technique is great in a duet situation, for accompanying any instrument or vocalist and in other instances where the guitar needs to create the rhythm, chords and bass part simultaneously. The essential technique can be summarized as a walking bass line (a bass note happening on every beat), simple chords which contain only the 3rd and 7th of each chord, (played on the "and of 1" and the "and of 3"). Let's separate each of these elements and see what techniques are used to construct them

First lets take a look at how to build a bass line for this technique. Each beat of the measure has a specific type of note that should be used. The first beat of each measure should contain the root of the chord (See Example 1). The 2nd quarter note of the measure should contain either a diatonic or chromatic note that leads by step into beat 3 (See Example 2). The 3rd quarter note of the measure should be either a chord tone (it's often the root) or a diatonic note of the chord (i.e. the root, 3rd, 5, or 7th),(See Example 3). The 4th quarter note of the measure should contain either a diatonic or chromatic note that leads by step into the next chord (See Example 4).

Example 1

Example 2

Example 3

Example 4

There are mainly only 3 chord types that are used in this technique; major 7th, minor 7th and dominant 7th, (if other chords are required only play the root, 3rd and 7th of the desired chord). The voicings for these chords can be found below. You will notice that there is only the root and the 3rd and 7th of the chord. All chords in a progression should be broken down into these basic chord types, and no tensions should be used for any chords. For example: a minor 7b5 chord should be changed to a minor 7th.

You will notice that the fingering seems a little strange. This suggested fingering allows you to play typical jazz progressions at very fast speeds. If you are playing a progression at a moderate tempo you can feel free to change the fingering. The chords are rhythmically placed on the "and of 1" and the "and of 3" (see page 85). Learn the progression on page 85 and then try writing your own bass and chord sequence using the information presented.

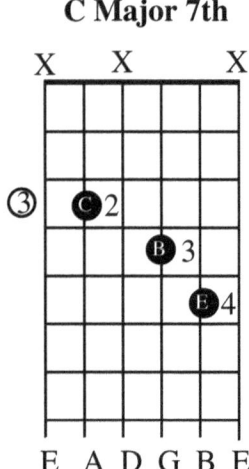
C Major 7th

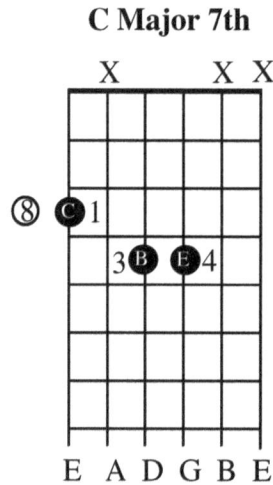
C Major 7th

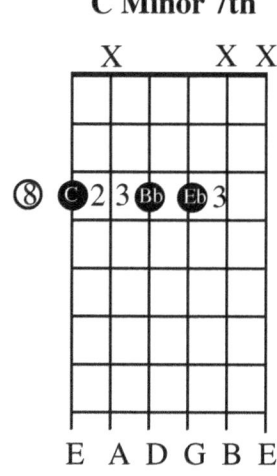
C Minor 7th

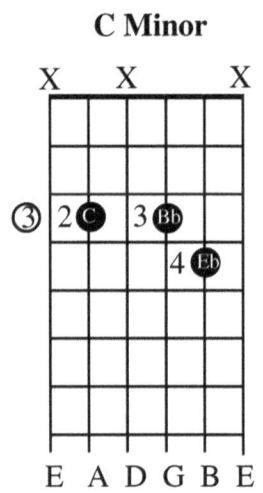
C Minor

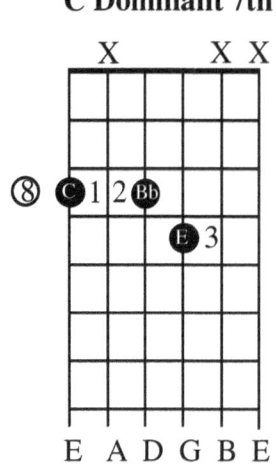
C Dominant 7th

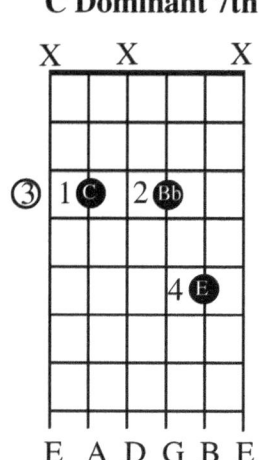
C Dominant 7th

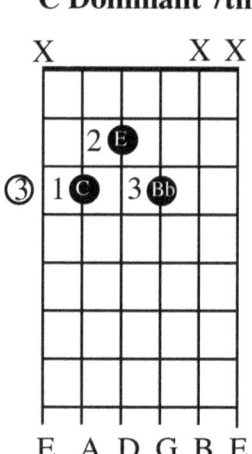
C Dominant 7th

C Blues Progression

Improvisation and Reharmonization Techniques

This next section present improvisation and reharmonization techniques commonly employed in contemporary music. Every style of music has typical types of improvisation/reharmonization techniques that are used. For example, rock mostly uses scales, i.e. pentatonic, blues and major modes, while traditional jazz uses both scale, arpeggios and approach notes. (See the "Music Workshop" at www.arnoldjazz.com for files for the 19 most used scales in improvisation and the basic 7th chord arpeggios). There are of course hundreds of other techniques available. We will concentrate on how to practice and develop your ability using only a few of the many possible improvisation and reharmonization techniques:

1. Modal Sequencing: An essential tool to developing and playing scales.

2. Approach Notes: A common technique employed in jazz melodies.

3. Two harmonization techniques commonly used in both chordal reharmonization and melodic content.

4. Hexatonics: An advanced improvisational technique which can be used to create "modern" melodic lines.

The last improvisational technique employing hexatonic scales is one that advanced students will find to be an interesting resource for more contemporary sounds.
Each concept presented will give you a detailed explanation of the technique, a technical method to practice the technique and possible applications in real music.
Along with studying the improvisational/reharmonizational concepts presented in this section it is highly recommended that you transcribe solos by various artists so you can really internalize the style. Whether it's Jimi Hendrix or Charlie Parker you need to experience the music first hand.

Modal Sequencing

Learning all your modes is a big job on the guitar. There are 22 different scales that are most commonly used in improvisation. All these scales need to be learned in all keys in order for you to be prepared for most situations that arise. Each scale needs to be learned in all possible positions on the guitar fretboard. An example of this can be seen on page 65. Organizing this job is important to getting the most out of each scale. The following schedule will help you organize this task.

1. Start with a major mode. Learn this scale in every position on the guitar thinking the notes/degrees rather than the fingering pattern (see page 65 for a major scale). You may also want to play your scales up and down each string fingering them in groups of threes. Example 1 shows you a C major scale played up the low E string. Playing scales up and down each string in all keys helps you break away from patterns and also helps you start to play in a more linear fashion on the guitar.

Example 1

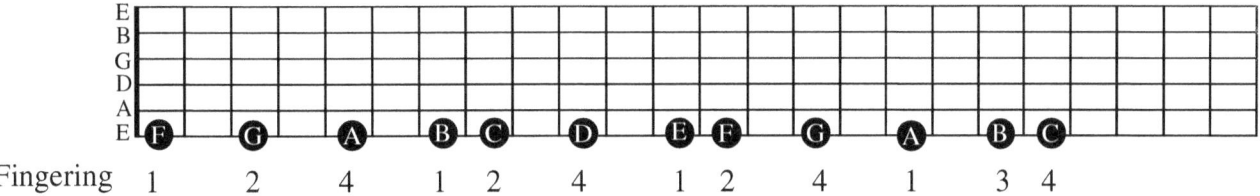

2. Continue working through all modes. You can organize this in two possible ways:

    a. Cycle each mode through all twelve keys moving Cycle 5 (see page 73 for an explanation of cycle 5).

    b. Learn all modes in one key. For example: learn the C major scale in all positions, then the C Dorian scale in all positions etc.

3. Apply each scale to songs and vamps so you can hear the scale in relationship to real music. (Muse-eek.com has audio files you can use to play with each scale.)

4. You should look at learning every mode in every key as just an introduction to mastering scales on the guitar. Much more work needs to be done to really know these scales and all their possibilities. Modal Sequencing is an excellent way of getting inside each scale. **Modal Sequencing is playing a melody through a scale in which it moves sequentially through each degree of the scale.** Example 2 on the next page shows you a simple two note sequence of a 3rd that is moved up and down a C major mode. By sequencing through all your modes you will build melodic ideas, chops, and a deeper understanding of each mode.

Example 2

Two Note Modal Sequencing

On page 89-92 examples of how you can organize modal sequencing are given. Sequential melodic patterns in music can be easily organized using a technique call permutation. For instance if you have two notes that you want to sequence through a scale there are only two possible ways you can do this. Example 1 and 2 show you an interval of a sixth and the two possible permutations.

Example 1
ascending sixth

Example 2
descending sixth

If we then sequence this sixth through a major scale we would get the two following possibilities or permutations:

Therefore any two note sequence has two possible melodic permutations. On page 89 I list all possible two note sequences within an octave, and a couple of examples of how they would be sequenced through a major scale. It is recommended that you play all your modes through all two note sequences.

Two Note Modal Sequencing

Two note ascending and descending thirds sequence.

Two note ascending and descending fourths sequence.

This sequencing and permutation idea can be applied to an almost infinite amount of possibilities, especially when different rhythm patterns are employed. One page 91-92 you will find three and four note sequencing examples. But you can take any group of notes and sequence them using the method presented here. Along with helping you learn your scales this modal sequencing/permutation idea can be a great resource for finding new ways to use old licks and developing solo ideas that are compositionally interrelated. This whole modal sequencing/permutation idea should be looked at as a life long way of organizing and working on scales. Pick a sequence and work it through every scale. This can take you many weeks but look at this as a life long journey into the world of scales and their melodic possibilities.

Three Note Modal Sequencing

Page 91 presents you with some 3 note sequencing possibilities. When you have a three note melody there are 6 ways to permutate it. Example 1 and 2 on page 91 show you two three note melodies and their corresponding permutations.

Four Note Modal Sequencing

Page 91 presents you with one four note sequencing possibility. When you have a four note melody there are 24 ways to permutate it. Example 1 and 2 on page 92 show you two four note melodies and there corresponding permutations.

Rhythmic Permutation of Modal Sequences

As you work with each sequence try playing it in different rhythms. For example play the sequences found on the bottom of page 92 in triplets rather than sixteenths. You will find by rhythmically altering even a simple sequence it can take on a whole new character.

Three Note Modal Sequencing

Example 1

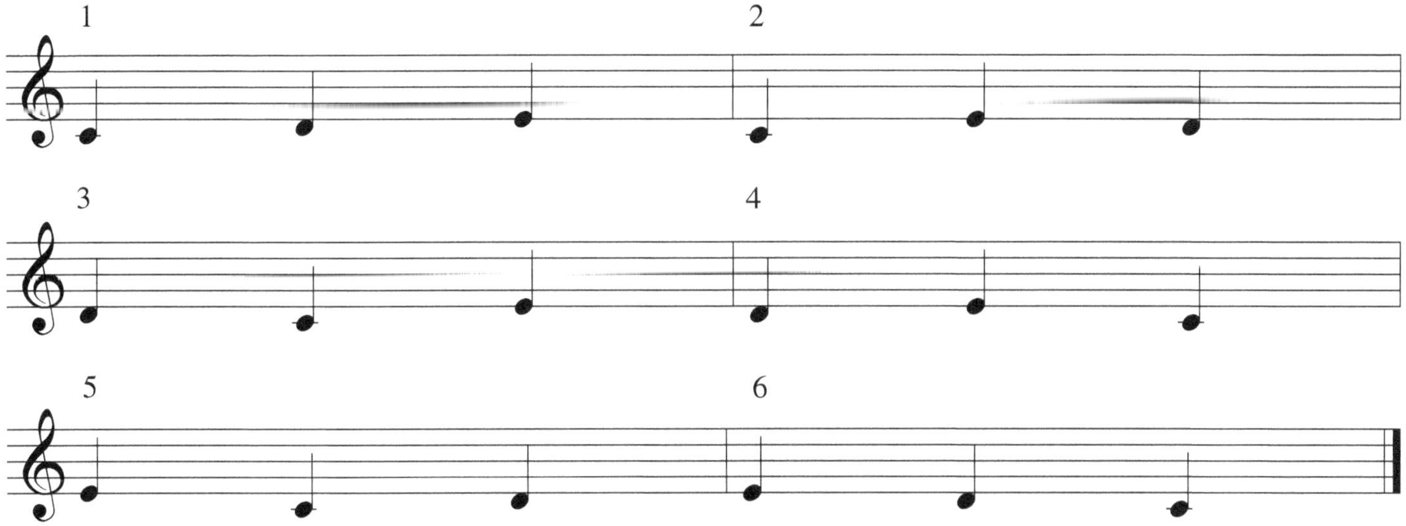

Example 2

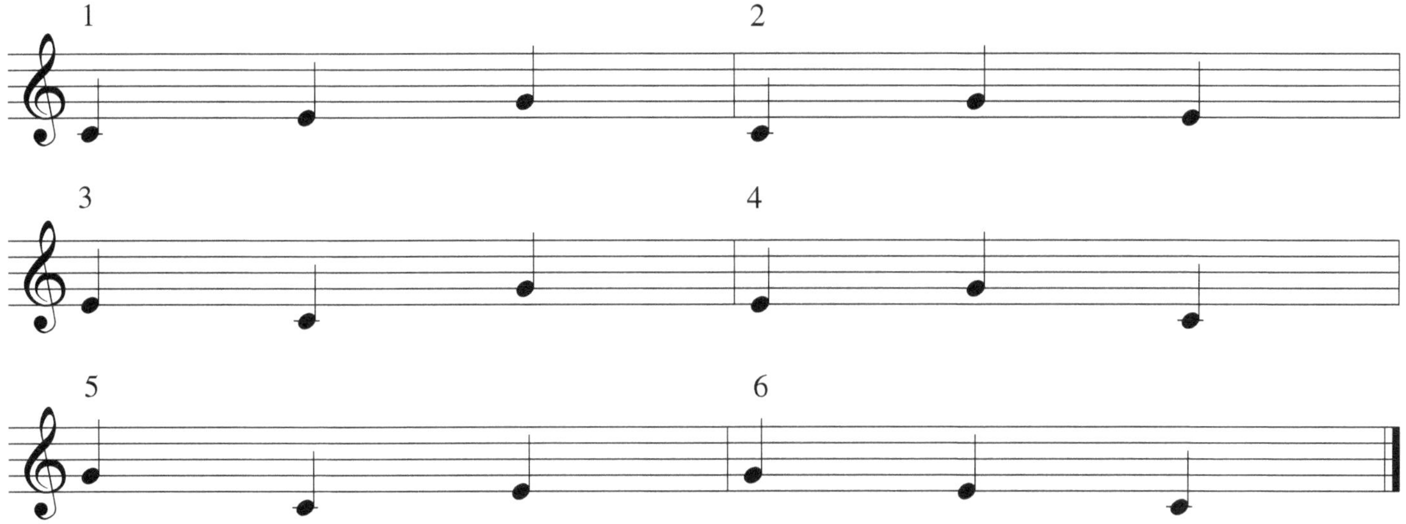

Example 1 melody sequenced through a major scale

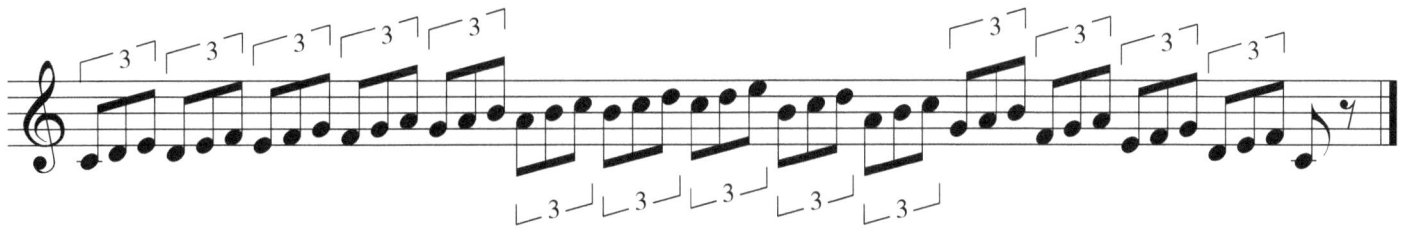

Example 2 melody sequenced through a major scale

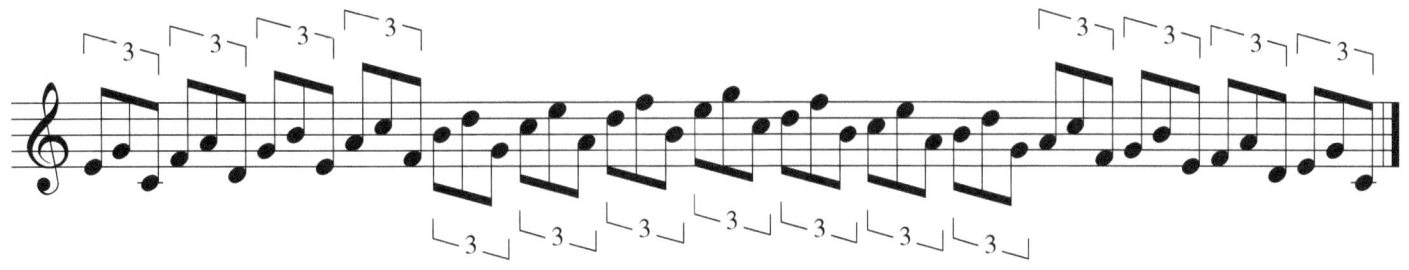

Four Note Modal Sequencing

Approach Notes

Approach notes are chromatic and/or diatonic notes which lead into a target note. This target note can be either a chord tone or a tension. Melodies using approach notes are one of the characteristic sounds of jazz. There are many different methods/styles of applying approach notes. These methods/styles can be broken down into three overall categories:

Approach tones that lead into:
1. Chord Tones.
2. Tensions
3. Tensions which when combined form chordal superimpositions.

Each of the three categories mentioned above create a specific sound that has been used in jazz during different stylistic periods. Approach tones leading into chord tones is a common BeBop technique especially when both Chromatic and Diatonic approaches are used. Approach tones leading into tension is common to the Modal Period of jazz but can also be found in the playing of contemporary jazz musicians. Approaches which form chordal superimpositions can be seen in abundance since the 1960's but certainly can also be traced back to pre-BeBop players such as Lester Young. The more advanced use of this technique however is more common to jazz from the 1960's on.

In order to develop an ability to use approach notes in the methods/style mentioned, a guitarist must first develop the technique and fretboard knowledge needed to use approach notes. This is a very difficult task for a guitarist. Because of the many possible ways to play any approach note figure and the number of possible places to play an arpeggio on the guitar the development of this technique is a very large undertaking but the rewards are huge. **Approach note lines form the basis of jazz and playing over chord changes.** Approach note lines are also very versatilegiving you many different types of melodies depending upon how you use them.

Lets first discuss how to tackle a technical exercises to gain theoritical and physical control of approach notes. Because approach notes commonly lead into chord tones it is important to first learn your arpeggios and then play approach note figures into these arpeggios. The following is a list of the 13 chord types.

Δ7	-7b5	-Δ7	Δ7#11
-7	°7	7#5	6
7	7sus4	Δ7#5	-6

You first need to learn the arpeggios associated with each of these chords. Fingerings for these arpeggios can be at the "Music Workshop" at www.arnoldjazz.com You need to learn these arpeggios in all keys and all inversions.

After you have learned the arpeggios you need to apply the approach notes figures to these arpeggios. Page 94-5 presents you with the 12 possible chromatic and diatonic approach note figures. You should at least apply the chromatic approach note figures to the chord arpeggios. I would suggest limiting the chord arpeggios types to 9 rather than 13. This will help to reduce the size of the exercise. Page 96 shows you how this should be organized.

Along with a technical study you should spend time writing lines employing approach notes. This should be done first on one chord vamps and then over common jazz tunes. Page 97 explains some of the possible ways approach notes can be used. It is also important to transcribe solos and see how players use approach notes. You will find a rich resource of ideas that musicians have developed over time using this technique.

12 Chromatic Approach Note Figures

Diatonic Approach Note Figures

Technical Exercise for Approach Notes

The exercise presented below should take 6 month to a year to complete. Although this may seem like a hugh task, the rewards are to numerous to mention here. Leave it said that you will have a command of chord arpeggios and will have developed an ability to physically approach any chord tone. As previously mentioned you should limit this exercise to 9 chord types rather than all 13. The following is a list of the chord types you should use:

Δ7	7sus4	dim7th
7	-Δ7	7#5
-7	-7b5	Δ7#5

Along with the example below you should approach the other chord tones i.e. 3rd 5th and 7th using the same method. Only use one approach at a time (if you are approaching the 3rd for example only approach the third every time you come to it in the arpeggio). These exercises should be played in all keys.

CΔ7 from the 5th degree

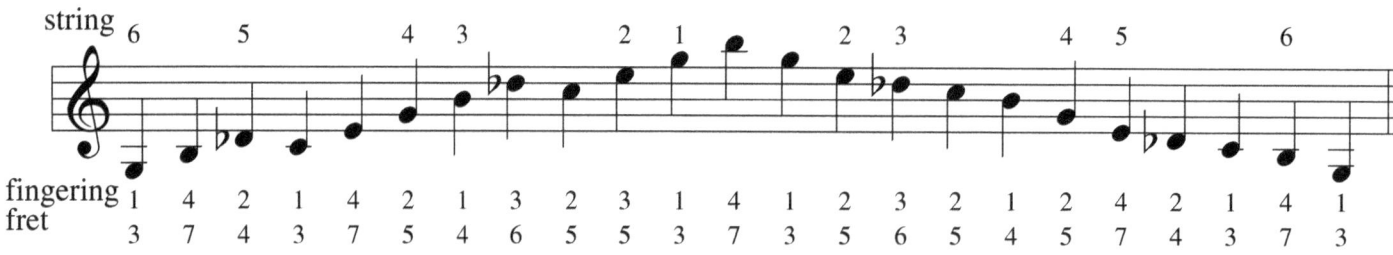

CΔ7 from the 7th degree

CΔ7 from the root

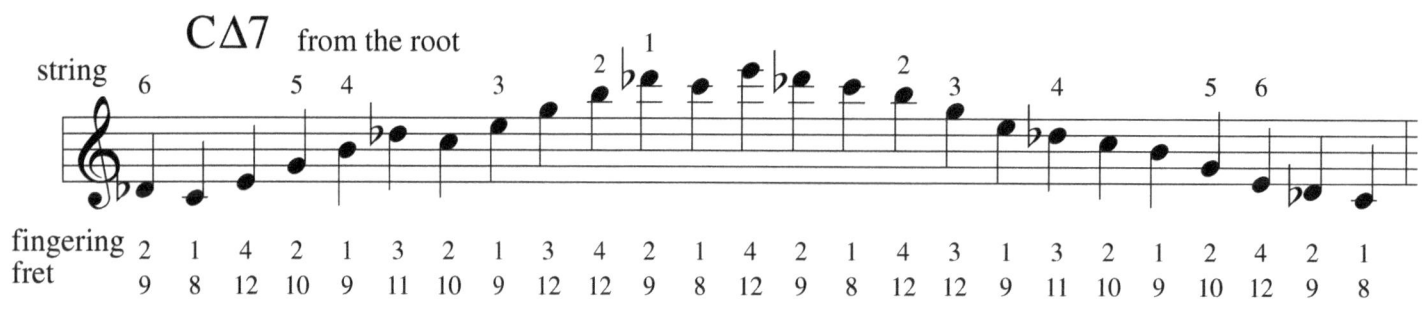

CΔ7 from the 3rd degree

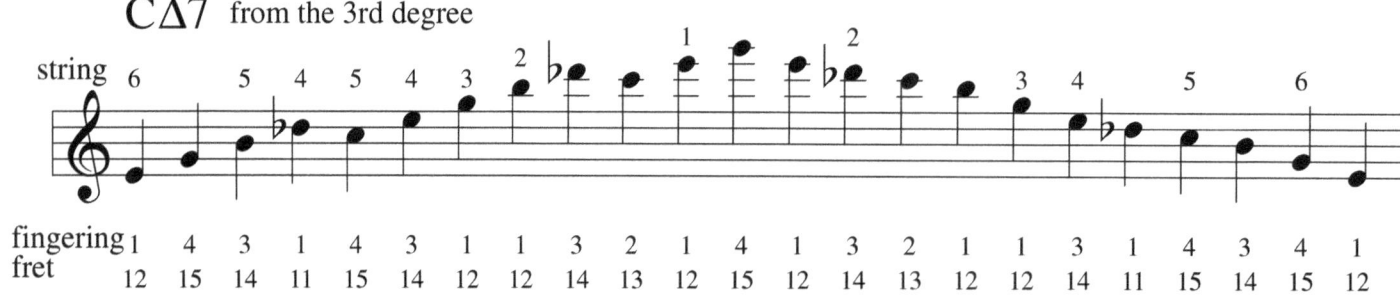

96

Possible uses of Approach Notes

Approach notes can be used in many different ways. Each method creates a different sound and therefore a different style. Each of the methods employed below should be studied and understood from a technical stand point and applied to chord vamps, and finally applied to common jazz progressions. The examples below are only a few of the ways approach notes can be applied.

A Diatonic approach can be used to approach chord tones which are commonly found on beats one and three

Example 1

A combination of diatonic and chromatic approaches can be used to approach chord tones which are placed on beats one and three.

Example 2

Chromatic and or diatonic approaches can be used to approach chord tones on every beat of the measure.

Example 3

Approach notes can be used to approach tensions. Tensions can be placed on beats one and three or on every beat.

Example 4

In example 5 the approaches are approaching the chord tones of a D7 chord (D, F#, A, C.) This works because all the chord tones of D7 are chord tones or available tensions on a CΔ7 chord.

Example 5

Chord Reharmonization

The first method of reharmonization is to add and subtract tensions. By learning the chord tones and tensions for each chord type (see page 38 for an example) you can add any of the available tensions. Therefore C dominant 7th could be C dominant b9 13 because b9 and 13 are available tensions for a C dominant chord.

Another method involves adding and subtracting chords to change the chord progression. Reharmonization by adding and subtracting chords has certain rules which govern which chords are substituted. This reharmonization theory is derived from the fact that our ear wants certain types of chords to resolve in certain ways and that some chords have an affinity with others because of their internal structure. A chord's tendency to move in a particular way is called it's "resolution tendency" One chord with a very strong resolution tendency is the dominant chord. Our ear wants to hear the dominant chord resolve in one of 3 ways: up a 4th (G7 to CΔ7), down a half step (Db7 to CΔ7), or up a whole step (Bb7 to CΔ7). These resolution tendencies of the dominant are also listed in order of the strongest resolution to the weakest (See Example 1). Therefore G7 to CΔ7 is the strongest and Bb7 to CΔ7 is the weakest. With this information we can take a blues and put the corresponding dominant structure before any chord. This dominant will then create a resolution to the chord that follows. The 12 bar blues found on page 82 does this in the 4th bar. You have an F#9 chord resolving down a half step to F9 in the 5th bar, then in bar 6 you have Bb13 resolving up a whole step to C13. Analyze the progressions found on page 77 and 82 and look for these reharmonizations. To review, we have **3 resolutions for a dominant chord, up a 4th, down a half step, or up a whole step**. Thinking of this another way, if we have CΔ7 we could put G7, Db7 or Bb7 in front of it for three possible reharmonizations.

Another common substitution is to place the related ii -7 in front of the 7th chord. For example if you have G7 to CΔ7 you can substitute D-7 to G7 to CΔ7 or ii-V-I. Using this idea we can use the -7 in front of our other two resolutions of the dominant Ab-7 to Db7 to CΔ7 and F-7 to Bb7 to CΔ7. Again these are listed in the order of strongest to weakest (See Example 1).

An example of this can be seen on page 77 with the F Minor Blues progression (bottom example). The Bb-7 in bar 5 resolves to the Eb9 in bar 6 which then resolves to the F-9 in bar 7. We can extend this theory to get even more possibilities for substitution. If CΔ7 can have 3 possible dominant chords: G7, Db7 and Bb7, **then these three dominants can be freely substituted for each other**. A progression of G7 to CΔ7 can just as well be Db7 to CΔ7 or Bb7 to CΔ7; you just have to keep in mind that some dominant resolutions are stronger than others. If we continue with this idea **all the -7's that can precede the dominant 7th can be freely substituted for each other**. Below is a list of all the possibilities starting from strongest to weakest.

Example 1

D-7 G7 CΔ7	Ab-7 Db7 CΔ7	F-7 Bb7 CΔ7	Strongest
D-7 Db7 CΔ7	Ab-7 G7 CΔ7	F-7 G7 CΔ7	
D-7 Bb7 CΔ7	Ab-7 Bb7 CΔ7	F-7 Db7 CΔ7	Weakest

An example of this type of substitution can be found on page 72. The F minor blues progression (bottom example) has a F-9 resolving to B7b913 in the 4th measure. This B7b913 then resolves to Bb-9 in the 5th measure.

Chords are also substituted because their internal structure is very similar. The most common example of this is the substitutions that occur within the diatonic chords of a key. If we look at the diatonic chords of C major we can see that C∆7, E-7 and A-7 all have many notes in common. D-7 and F∆7 also have many notes in common as does G7 and B-7b5. Our ear picks up on this and doesn't mind if we substitute these similar structures.

Diatonic 7th chords of C major

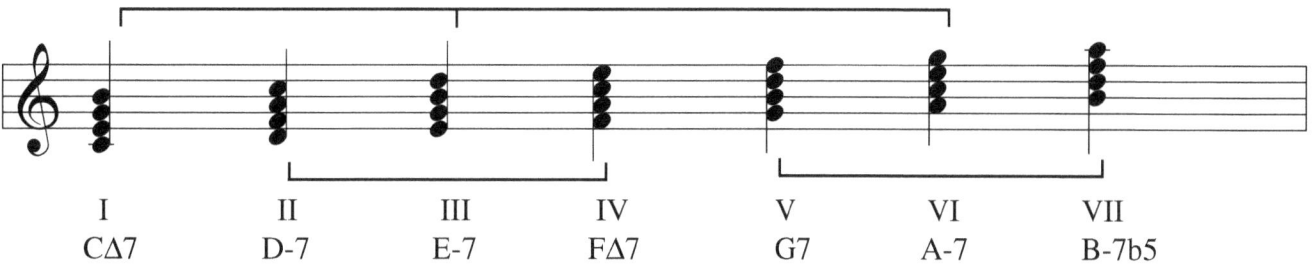

These three different groups of chords are commonly referred to as the tonic area (C∆7, E-7 and A-7), the subdominant area (D-7 and F∆7) and the dominant area (G7 and B-7b5). You will find many examples of this type of substitution in the rhythm changes progressions found in the "Chord Workbook for Guitar Volume One."

The next reharmonization technique expands on the principle that for every chord type there is a list of chord tones and available tensions that can be used. If we take all these notes and recombine them in different orders we will find many other chords. For example, C∆7 contains the chord tones 1,3,5,7 (C,E,G,B) and has the available tension of 9,#11,13 (D,F#,A). If we recombine these notes we find that C,E,G,A, forms a C6. D,F#,A,C forms a D7 chord. E,G,B,D, forms an E-7 chord. F#,A,C,E forms a F#-7b5 chord. Therefore you can use these chords as replacements for the C∆7. Furthermore many chord voicings that do not contain the complete chord structure will also work as a substitution, because the notes contained in their specific voicings all have notes that are available. For example a four note voicing of an Ab∆7#5add#11 would have to contain C,E,G, and D with the root left out. This Ab∆7#5add#11 specific voicing would work as a substitute for C∆7 because all of the notes present in the chord are available notes on a C∆7 chord. You can see that this opens up a whole new world of sound possibilities. With this new world comes the task of creatively and musically applying these chords to a given situation. Extreme care must be taken when using these reharmonized chords. Each musical situation is unique so you must use your ear and common sense when attempting to use these reharmonizations. The blues progression found on page 82 gives you an example of a blues progression that has been reharmonized using this technique.

Hexatonics

Hexatonics is the one of the more advanced contemporary techniques employed by modern improvisers. This improvisational technique can be found in the playing of McCoy Tyner, Chick Corea, Herbie Hancock, Dave Liebman, and Michael Brecker. First we will discuss how this technique works. Then technical exercises will be introduced to help you gain command over this technique. After that, other applications of this technique will be explored.

The overall concept of hexatonics is to divide the hexatonic scale (six note scale) into two groups of 3 notes. Example 1 shows you a common hexatonic scale. Example 2 shows you this same hexatonic scale divide up into two major triads.

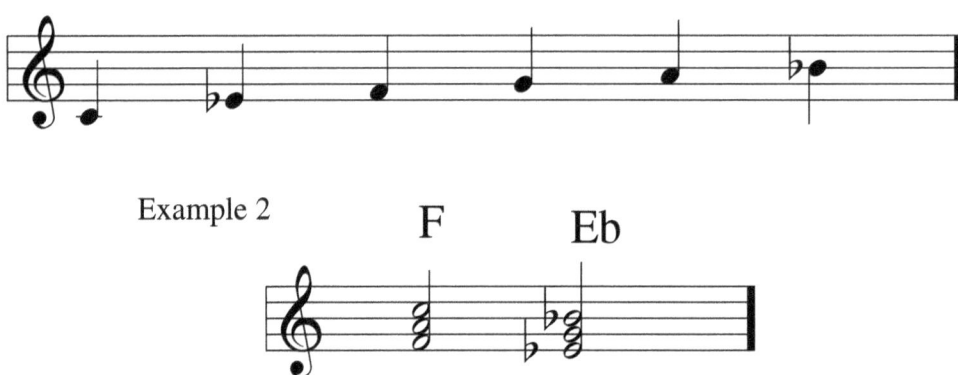

The next step in this technique is to alternate between these two triads. Commonly groups of two, three or four eighth notes worth of time are used to "break up" the triads. Example 3 below shows you two melodies employing this technique.

Check out McCoy Tyner's composition "Passion Dance" for a good example of this hexatonic scale.

Technical Exercise for Hexatonics

Applying hexatonics on the guitar requires first learning your triads in every position and developing the ability to move back and forth between these two triads. The exercise below will help you gain control of this technique. Practice this exercise in all keys.

Other Tertial* Hexatonic Groupings

Other Hexatonic scales can be used to create new sounding melodies. Example 1 shows a hexatonic scale divided up into a major and an augmented triad.

Example 1

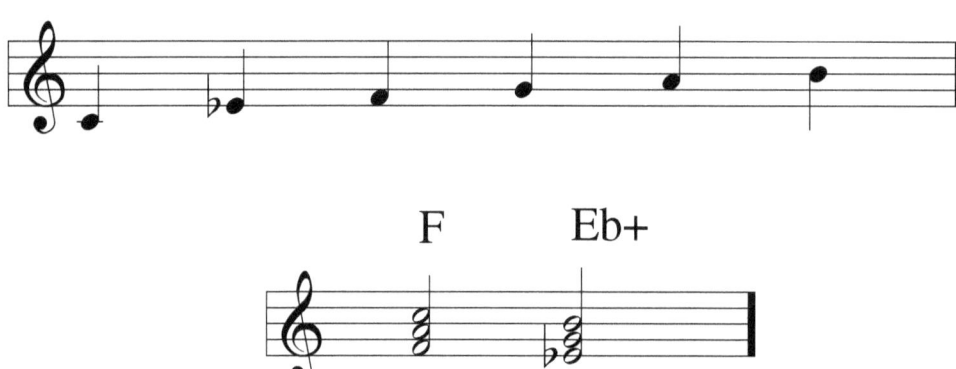

Example 2 shows you some melodies using the F and E+ triads.

Example 2

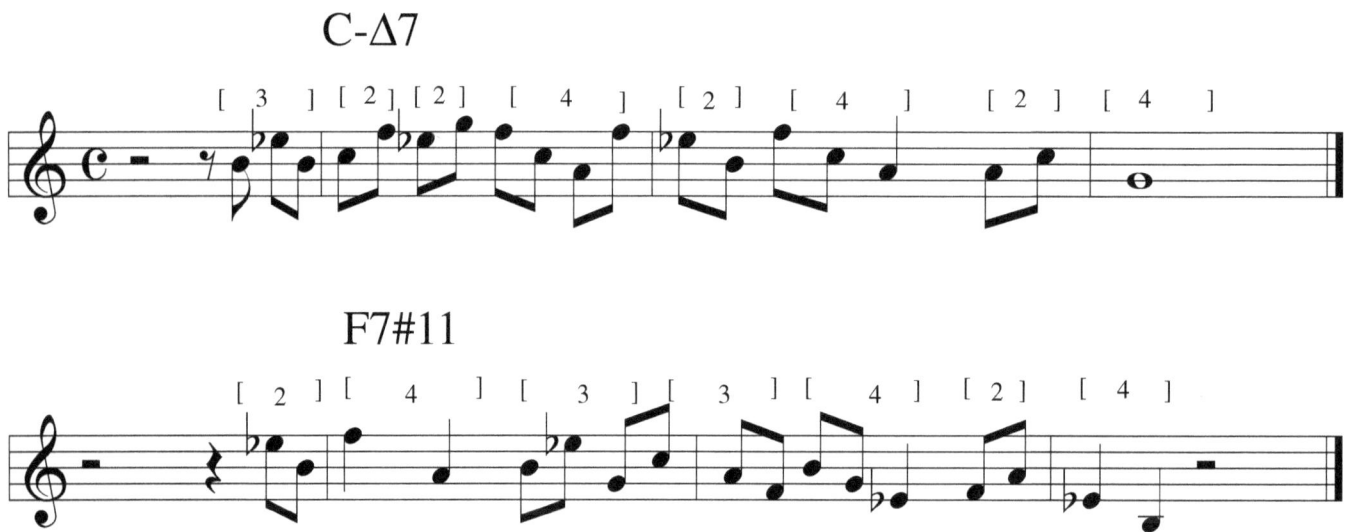

also try these melodies on the chords: D7sus4b9, EbΔ7#5, G7b13, A-7b5 natural 9, B7 Altered.

* Tertial means the structure is built in 3rds.

Technical Exercise for Hexatonics

Apply this hexatonic in the same way as the previous exercise. Practice in all keys.

Non-Tertial Hexatonics

Hexatonics can also be applied by choosing non-tertial (not built in thirds) based triads. Example 1 shows the same hexatonics as the same scale found on page 100 but the triads are non-tertial.

Example 1

* An explanation of integer notation can be found on page 107.

Example 2 shows you some melodies using two 027's

also try these melodies on the following chords:
D7sus4*
D-7 Phrygian**
EbΔ7
F7sus4
F-7
G-7 aeolian**
AbΔ7
A-7b5 Locrian**
A7sus4**
Bb7sus4
BbΔ7**

* This is used in a situation where altered tensions sound good.
** keep in mind here you may be dealing with avoid notes. This will all depend on the musical context.

Technical Exercise for Hexatonics

Apply this hexatonic in the same way as previously.   Practice this exercise in all keys.

Hexatonics as an Improvisational/Compositional Tool

Hexatonics create a remarkably fresh sound for improvisation. Hexatonics can also be used as a compositional tool as in the previously mentioned "Passion Dance" by McCoy Tyner. Non-tertial hexatonic groups are a very rich resource for improvisation and composition. Page 104 presented only one such non-tertial combination. An interesting use of this 027 can be found in the composition "A Day in the Badlands" which is on my first CD entitled "Blue Eleven." On this same CD you will find examples of other non-tertial hexatonics. Listen to the 4 "Variations" where I employ a 015 non-tertial hexatonic. Further listening recommendations include my 2nd CD entitled "A Few Dozen" where I employ 103, 014 and 016, 027 combinations. The "A Few Dozen" CD also includes in the liner notes a brief description of the non-tertial hexatonics used for each tune. The previously mentioned tunes also incorporate an interesting twist on hexatonics. See below for a short explanation.

Further Applications of Hexatonics

An interesting relationship exists between hexatonics and 12 Tone (serial) composition. Because there are 12 notes all together in western music a hexatonic evenly divides these 12 possible notes into two groups. It is possible to use this as a compositional tool to create interesting music. If we use our 027 presented on page 104 we will find that the 027 can be used to symmetrically divide up all 12 notes. Example 1 shows you four 027's which when combined create a 12 tone grouping.

Example 1

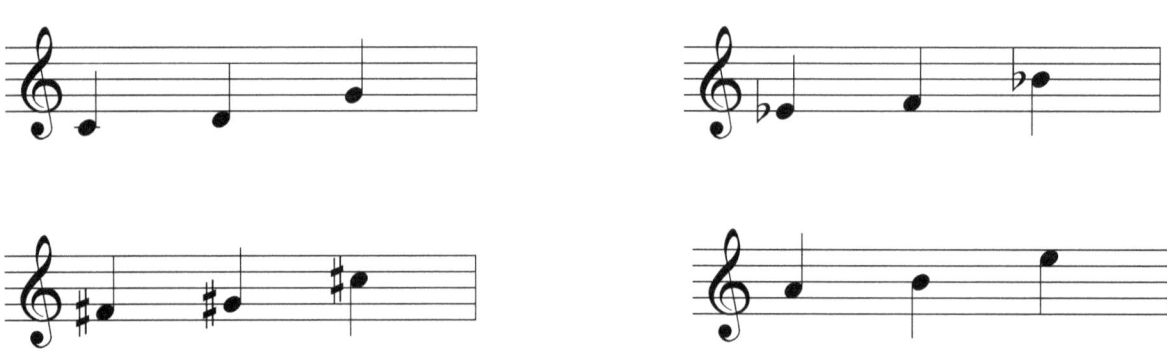

The same technique we used to alternate between two triads can be used to alternate between four non-tertial triads (also called trichords) This will create 12 tone lines when all 3 notes of each group are used. You can also create melodies when just employing the two, three or four eighth notes worth of time pattern previously used to "break up" the 3 note groups. Example 2 below shows a melody employing this technique.

Example 2

All the compositions on the previously mentioned CD "A Few Dozen" employ this technique for composition and improvisation. There is also another example of this technique in the "Music Workshop, Further Investigations" section at www.arnoldjazz.com

Integer Notation

When discussing twentieth century theoretical concepts integer notation is used in place of the traditional interval system. The following is a list of the integers used for intervals.

traditional name	Number of semitones
unison	0
minor 2nd	1
major 2nd, diminished 3rd	2
minor 3rd, augmented 2nd	3
major 3rd, diminished 4th	4
augmented 3rd, perfect 4th	5
augmented 4th, diminished 5th	6
perfect 5th, diminished 6th	7
augmented 5th, diminshed 6th	8
major 6th, diminshed 7th	9
augmented 6th, minor 7th	10
major 7th	11
octave	12
minor 9th	13
major 9th	14
minor 10th	15
major 10th	16

Therefore, if you had C, D and G, this group of notes (better known as a "pitch class set") would be called 027. 0 representing the C, 2 representing the interval of a major 2nd between C and D, and 7 representing the interval of a perfect 5 between C and G.

example 1

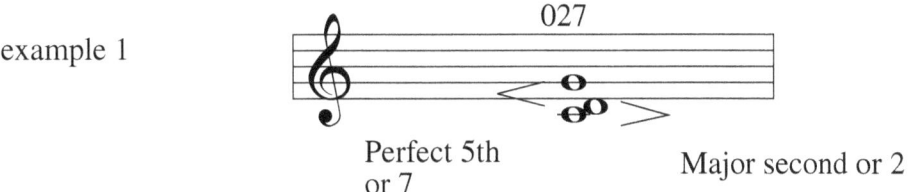

Perfect 5th or 7

Major second or 2

Any group of notes is always reduced to its smallest interval order, better known as its "prime form." For example: D, G and C would be 0510

example 2

Minor 7th or 10

Perfect 4th or 5

but, if we rearrange the notes into its smallest interval combination we will find that D to G to C is better expressed as C to D to G or 027. See example 1.

By always reducing a pitch class set to its prime form you can easily organize and see relationships within any group of notes.

Books Available From
Muse Eek Publishing Company

The Bruce Arnold series of instruction books for guitar are the result of 20 years of teaching. Mr. Arnold, who teaches at New York University and Princeton University has listened to the questions and problems of his students, and written forty books addressing the needs of the beginning to advanced student. Written in a direct, friendly and practical manner, each book is structured in such as way as to enable a student to understand, retain and apply musical information. In short, <u>these books teach</u>.

1st Steps for a Beginning Guitarist
Spiral Bound ISBN 1890944-90-4   Perfect Bound ISBN 1890944-93-9

"1st Steps for a Beginning Guitarist" is a comprehensive method for guitar students who have no prior musical training. Whether you are playing acoustic, electric or twelve-string guitar, this book will give you the information you need, and trouble shoot the various pitfalls that can hinder the self-taught musician. Includes pictures, videos and audio in the form of midifiles and mp3's.

Chord Workbook for Guitar Volume 1 (2nd edition)
Spiral Bound ISBN 0-9648632-1-9   Perfect Bound ISBN 1890944-50-5

<u>A consistent seller</u>, this book addresses the needs of the beginning through intermediate student. The beginning student will learn chords on the guitar, and a section is also included to help learn the basics of music theory. Progressions are provided to help the student apply these chords to common sequences. The more advanced student will find the reharmonization section to be an invaluable resource of harmonic choices. Information is given through musical notation as well as tablature.

Chord Workbook for Guitar Volume 2 (2nd edition)
Spiral Bound ISBN 0-9648632-3-5   Perfect Bound ISBN 1890944-51-3

This book is the Rosetta Stone of pop/jazz chords, and is geared to the intermediate to advanced student. These are the chords that any serious student bent on a musical career must know. Unlike other books which simply give examples of isolated chords, this unique book provides a comprehensive series of progressions and chord combinations which are immediately applicable to both composition and performance.

Music Theory Workbook for Guitar Series

The world's most popular instrument, the guitar, is not taught in our public schools. In addition, it is one of the hardest on which to learn the basics of music. As a result, it is frequently difficult for the serious guitarist to get a firm foundation in theory.

Theory Workbook for Guitar Volume 1
Spiral Bound ISBN   0-9648632-4-3   Perfect Bound ISBN 1890944-52-1

This book provides real hands-on application of intervals and chords. A theory section written in concise and easy to understand language prepares the student for all exercises. Worksheets are given that quiz a student about intervals and chord construction using staff notation and guitar tablature. Answers are supplied in the back of the book enabling a student to work without a teacher.

Theory Workbook for Guitar Volume 2
Spiral Bound ISBN   0-9648632-5-1   Perfect Bound ISBN 1890944-53-X

This book provides real hands-on application for 22 different scale types. A theory section written in concise and easy to understand language prepares the student for all exercises. Worksheets are given that quiz a student about scale construction using staff notation and guitar tablature. Answers are supplied in the back of the book enabling a student to work without a teacher. Audio files are also available on the muse-eek.com website to facilitate practice and improvisation with all the scales presented.

Rhythm Book Series

These books are a breakthrough in music instruction, using the internet as a teaching tool! Audio files of all the exercises are easily downloaded from the internet.

Rhythm Primer
Spiral Bound ISBN 0-890944-03-3   Perfect Bound ISBN 1890944-59-9

This 61 page book concentrates on all basic rhythms using four rhythmic levels. All examples use one pitch, allowing the student to focus completely on time and rhythm. All exercises can be downloaded from the internet to facilitate learning. See http://www.muse-eek.com for details

Rhythms Volume 1
Spiral Bound ISBN 0-9648632-7-8   Perfect Bound ISBN 1890944-55-6

This 120 page book concentrates on eighth note rhythms and is a thesaurus of rhythmic patterns. All examples use one pitch, allowing the student to focus completely on time and rhythm. All exercises can be downloaded from the internet to facilitate learning. See http://www.muse-eek.com for details.

Rhythms Volume 2
Spiral Bound ISBN   0-9648632-8-6   Perfect Bound ISBN 1890944-56-4

This volume concentrates on sixteenth note rhythms, and is a 108 page thesaurus of rhythmic patterns. All examples use one pitch, allowing the student to focus completely on time and rhythm. All exercises can be downloaded from the internet to facilitate learning. See http://www.muse-eek.com for details.

Rhythms Volume 3
Spiral Bound ISBN   0-890944-04-1   Perfect Bound ISBN 1890944-57-2

This volume concentrates on thirty second note rhythms, and is a 102 page thesaurus of rhythmic patterns. All examples use one pitch, allowing the student to focus completely on time and rhythm. All exercises can be downloaded from the internet to facilitate learning. See http://www.muse-eek.com for details.

Odd Meters Volume 1
Spiral Bound ISBN 0-9648632-9-4   Perfect Bound ISBN 1890944-58-0

This book applies both eighth and sixteenth note rhythms to odd meter combinations. All examples use one pitch, allowing the student to focus completely on time and rhythm. Exercises can be downloaded from the internet to facilitate learning. This 100 page book is an essential sight reading tool.
See http://www.muse-eek.com for details.

Contemporary Rhythms Volume 1
Spiral Bound ISBN 1-890944-27-0   Perfect Bound ISBN 1890944-84-X

This volume concentrates on eight note rhythms and is a thesaurus of rhythmic patterns. Each exercise uses one pitch which allows the student to focus completely on time and rhythm. Exercises use modern innovations common to twentieth century notation, thereby familiarizing the student with the most sophisticated systems likely to be encountered in the course of a musical career. All exercises can be downloaded from the internet to facilitate learning. See http://www.muse-eek.com for details.

Contemporary Rhythms Volume 2
Spiral Bound ISBN 1-890944-28-9   Perfect Bound ISBN 1890944-85-8

This volume concentrates on sixteenth note rhythms and is a thesaurus of rhythmic patterns. Each exercise uses one pitch which allows the student to focus completely on time and rhythm. Exercise use modern innovations common to twentieth century notation, thereby familiarizing the student with the most sophisticated systems likely to be encountered in the course of a musical career. All exercises can be downloaded from the internet to facilitate learning. See http://www.muse-eek.com for details.

Independence Volume 1
Spiral Bound ISBN 1-890944-00-9   Perfect Bound ISBN 1890944-83-1

This 51 page book is designed for pianists, stick and touchstyle guitarists, percussionists and anyone who wishes to develop the rhythmic independence of their hands. This volume concentrates on quarter, eighth and sixteenth note rhythms and is a thesaurus of rhythmic patterns. The exercises in this book gradually incorporate more and more complex rhythmic patterns making it an excellent tool for both the beginning and the advanced student.

Other Guitar Study Aids

Right Hand Technique for Guitar Volume 1
Spiral Bound ISBN 0-9648632-6-X   Perfect Bound ISBN 1890944-54-8

Here's a breakthrough in music instruction, using the internet as a teaching tool! This book gives a concise method for developing right hand technique on the guitar, one of the most overlooked and under-addressed aspects of learning the instrument. The simplest, most basic movements are used to build fatigue-free technique. Exercises can be downloaded from the internet to facilitate learning. See http://www.muse-eek.com for details.

Single String Studies Volume One
Spiral Bound ISBN 1-890944-01-7   Perfect Bound ISBN 1890944-62-9

This book is an excellent learning tool for both the beginner who has no experience reading music on the guitar, and the advanced student looking to improve their ledger line reading and general knowledge of each string of the guitar. Each exercise concentrates the students attention on one string at a time. This allows a familiarity to form between the written pitch and where it can be found on the guitar along with improving one's "feel" for jumping linearly across the fretboard. Exercises can be downloaded from the internet to facilitate learning. See http://www.muse-eek.com for details.

Single String Studies Volume Two
Spiral Bound ISBN 1-890944-05-X   Perfect Bound ISBN 1890944-64-5

This book is a continuation of Volume One, but using non-diatonic notes. Volume Two helps the intermediate and advanced student improve their ledger line reading and general knowledge of each string of the guitar. Each exercise concentrates the students attention on one string at a time. This allows a familiarity to form between the written pitch and where it can be found on the guitar along with improving one's "feel" for jumping linearly across the fretboard. Exercises can be downloaded from the internet to facilitate learning. See http://www.muse-eek.com for details.

Single String Studies Volume One (Bass Clef)
Spiral Bound ISBN 1-890944-02-5   Perfect Bound ISBN 1890944-63-7

This book is an excellent learning tool for both the beginner who has no experience reading music on the bass guitar, and the advanced student looking to improve their ledger line reading and general knowledge of each string of the bass. Each exercise concentrates a students attention of one string at a time. This allows a familiarity to form between the written pitch and where it can be found on the bass along with improving one's "feel" for jumping linearly across the fretboard. Exercises can be downloaded from the internet to facilitate learning. See http://www.muse-eek.com for details.

Single String Studies Volume Two (Bass Clef)
Spiral Bound ISBN 1-890944-06-8   Perfect Bound ISBN 1890944-65-3

This book is a continuation of Volume One, but using non-diatonic notes. Volume Two helps the intermediate and advanced student improve their ledger line reading and general knowledge of each string of the bass. Each exercise concentrates the students attention on one string at a time. This allows a familiarity to form between the written pitch and where it can be found on the bass along with improving one's "feel" for jumping linearly across the fretboard. Exercises can be downloaded from the internet to facilitate learning. See http://www.muse-eek.com for details.

Guitar Clinic
Spiral Bound ISBN 1-890944-45-9   Perfect Bound ISBN 1890944-86-6

Guitar Clinic" contains techniques and exercises Mr. Arnold uses in the clinics and workshops he teaches around the U.S.. Much of the material in this book is culled from Mr. Arnold's educational series, over thirty books in all. The student wishing to expand on his or her studies will find suggestions within the text as to which of Mr. Arnold's books will best serve their specific needs. Topics covered include: how to read music, sight reading, reading rhythms, music theory, chord and scale construction, modal sequencing, approach notes, reharmonization, bass and chord comping, and hexatonic scales.

Sight Singing and Ear Training Series

The world is full of ear training and sight reading books, so why do we need more?
This sight singing and ear training series uses a different method of teaching relative pitch sight singing and ear training. The success of this method has been remarkable. Along with a new method of ear training these books also use CDs and the internet as a teaching tool! Audio files of all the exercises are easily downloaded from the internet at www.muse-eek.com By combining interactive audio files with a new approach to ear training a student's progress is limited only by their willingness to practice!

A Fanatic's Guide to Ear Training and Sight Singing
Spiral Bound ISBN 1-890944-19-X   Perfect Bound ISBN 1890944-75-0

This book and CD present a method for developing good pitch recognition through sight singing. This method differs from the myriad of other sight singing books in that it develops the ability to identify and name all twelve pitches within a key center. Through this method a student gains the ability to identify sound based on it's relationship to a key and not the relationship of one note to another (i.e. interval training as commonly taught in many texts). All note groupings from one to six notes are presented giving the student a thesaurus of basic note combinations which develops sight singing and note recognition to a level unattainable before this Guide's existence.

Key Note Recognition
Spiral Bound ISBN 1-890944-30-0   Perfect Bound ISBN 1890944-77-7

This book and CD present a method for developing the ability to recognize the function of any note against a key. This method is a must for anyone who wishes to sound one note on an instrument or voice and instantly know what key a song is in. Through this method a student gains the ability to identify a sound based on its relationship to a key and not the relationship of one note to another (i.e. interval training as commonly taught in many texts). Key Center Recognition is a definite requirement before proceeding to two note ear training.

LINES Volume One: Sight Reading and Sight Singing Exercises
Spiral Bound ISBN 1-890944-09-2   Perfect Bound ISBN 1890944-76-9

This book can be used for many applications. It is an excellent source for easy half note melodies that a beginner can use to learn how to read music or for sight singing slightly chromatic lines. An intermediate or advanced student will find exercises for multi-voice reading. These exercises can also be used for multi-voice ear training. The book has the added benefit in that all exercises can be heard by downloading the audio files for each example. See http://www.muse-eek.com for details.

Ear Training ONE NOTE: Beginning Level
Spiral Bound ISBN 1-890944-12-2   Perfect Bound ISBN 1890944-66-1

This is a new method for developing instantaneous recognition of pitches within a key. This contextual-based ear training differs from interval based training by instilling a sense of key relationship; that is, a note is identified by it's characteristic sound within a key, and not by its distance from another note. This method has been used with great success and is now finally available on CD. There are three levels available depending on the student's ability. This beginning level is recommended for students who have little or no music training. A Complete Method book containing the Ear Training One Note Beginning, Intermediate and Advanced levels along with three accompanying CDs is also available for those students wishing to have a complete set of books and CDs under one cover.

Ear Training ONE NOTE: Intermediate Level
Spiral Bound ISBN 1-890944-13-0   Perfect Bound ISBN 1890944-67-X

This is a new method for developing instantaneous recognition of pitches within a key. This contextual-based ear training differs from interval based training by instilling a sense of key relationship; that is, a note is identified by it's characteristic sound within a key, and not by its distance from another note. This method has been used with great success and is now finally available on CD. There are three levels available depending on the student's ability. This intermediate level is recommended for students who have had some music training but still find their skills need more development. A Complete Method book containing the Ear Training One Note Beginning, Intermediate and Advanced levels along with three accompanying CDs is also available for those students wishing to have a complete set of books and CDs under one cover.

Ear Training ONE NOTE: Advanced Level
Spiral Bound ISBN 1-890944-14-9   Perfect Bound ISBN 1890944-68-8

This is a new method for developing instantaneous recognition of pitches within a key. This contextual-based ear training differs from interval based training by instilling a sense of key relationship; that is, a note is identified by it's characteristic sound within a key, and not by its distance from another note. This method has been used with great success and is now finally available on CD. There are three levels available depending on the student's ability. This advanced level is recommended for advanced music students or those who have worked with the intermediate level and now wish to perfect their skills. A Complete Method book containing the Ear Training One Note Beginning, Intermediate and Advanced levels along with three accompanying CDs is also available for those students wishing to have a complete set of books and CDs under one cover.

Ear Training ONE NOTE: Complete Method
Spiral Bound ISBN 1-890944-47-5   Perfect Bound ISBN 1890944-48-3

This is a new method for developing instantaneous recognition of pitches within a key. This contextual-based ear training differs from interval based training by instilling a sense of key relationship; that is, a note is identified by it's characteristic sound within a key, and not by its distance from another note. This Complete Method book contains the Ear Training One Note Beginning, Intermediate and Advanced levels along with three accompanying CDsand is available for those students who wish to have a complete set of books and CDs under one cover.

Ear Training TWO NOTE: Beginning Level Volume One
Spiral Bound ISBN 1-890944-31-9   Perfect Bound ISBN 1890944-69-6

This Book and Audio CD continues the method of developing relative pitch ear training as set forth in the "Ear Training, One Note" series. There are six volumes in the beginning level series. Through practice, the student eventually gains the ability to recognize the key and the names of any two notes played simultaneously. Volume One concentrates on 5ths. Prerequisite: a strong grasp of the One Note method.

Ear Training TWO NOTE: Beginning Level Volume Two
Spiral Bound ISBN 1-890944-32-7   Perfect Bound ISBN 1890944-70-X

This Book and Audio CD continues the method of developing relative pitch ear training as set forth in the "Ear Training, One Note" series. There are six volumes in the beginning level series. Through practice, the student eventually gains the ability to recognize the key and the names of any two notes played simultaneously. Volume Two concentrates on 3rds. Prerequisite: a strong grasp of the One Note method.

Ear Training TWO NOTE: Beginning Level Volume Three
Spiral Bound ISBN 1-890944-33-5   Perfect Bound ISBN 1890944-71-8

This Book and Audio CD continues the method of developing relative pitch ear training as set forth in the "Ear Training, One Note" series. There are six volumes in the beginning level series. Through practice, the student eventually gains the ability to recognize the key and the names of any two notes played simultaneously. Volume Three concentrates on 6ths. Prerequisite: a strong grasp of the One Note method.

Ear Training TWO NOTE: Beginning Level Volume Four
Spiral Bound ISBN 1-890944-34-3   Perfect Bound ISBN 1890944-72-6

This Book and Audio CD continues the method of developing relative pitch ear training as set forth in the "Ear Training, One Note" series. There are six volumes in the beginning level series. Through practice, the student eventually gains the ability to recognize the key and the names of any two notes played simultaneously. Volume Four concentrates on 4ths. Prerequisite: a strong grasp of the One Note method.

Ear Training TWO NOTE: Beginning Level Volume Five
Spiral Bound ISBN 1-890944-35-1   Perfect Bound ISBN 1890944-73-4

This Book and Audio CD continues the method of developing relative pitch ear training as set forth in the "Ear Training, One Note" series. There are six volumes in the beginning level series. Through practice, the student eventually gains the ability to recognize the key and the names of any two notes played simultaneously. Volume Five concentrates on 2nds. Prerequisite: a strong grasp of the One Note method.

Ear Training TWO NOTE: Beginning Level Volume Six
Spiral Bound ISBN 1-890944-36-X   Perfect Bound ISBN 1890944-74-2

This Book and Audio CD continues the method of developing relative pitch ear training as set forth in the "Ear Training, One Note" series. There are six volumes in the beginning level series. Through practice, the student eventually gains the ability to recognize the key and the names of any two notes played simultaneously. Volume Six concentrates on 7ths. Prerequisite: a strong grasp of the One Note method.

Comping Styles Series

This series is built on the progressions found in Chord Workbook Volume One. Each book covers a specific style of music and presents exercises to help a guitarist, bassist or drummer master that style. Audio CDs are also available so a student can play along with each example and really get "into the groove."

Comping Styles for the Guitar Volume Two FUNK
Spiral Bound ISBN 1-890944-07-6   Perfect Bound ISBN 1890944-60-2

This volume teaches a student how to play guitar or piano in a funk style. 36 Progressions are presented: 12 keys of a Major and Minor Blues plus 12 keys of Rhythm Changes A different groove is presented for each exercise giving the student a wide range of funk rhythms to master. An Audio CD is also included so a student can play along with each example and really get "into the groove." The audio CD contains "trio" versions of each exercise with Guitar, Bass and Drums.

Comping Styles for the Bass Volume Two FUNK
Spiral Bound ISBN 1-890944-08-4   Perfect Bound ISBN 1890944-61-0

This volume teaches a student how to play bass in a funk style. 36 Progressions are presented: 12 keys of a Major and Minor Blues plus 12 keys of Rhythm Changes A different groove is presented for each exercise giving the student a wide range of funk rhythms to master. An Audio CD is also included so a student can play along with each example and really get "into the groove." The audio CD contains "trio" versions of each exercise with Guitar, Bass and Drums.

Bass Lines: Learning and Understanding the Jazz-Blues Bass Line
Spiral Bound ISBN 1-890944-94-7   Perfect Bound ISBN 1890944-95-5

This book covers the basics of bass line construction. A theoretical guide to building bass lines is presented along with 36 chord progressions utilizing the twelve keys of a Major and Minor Blues, plus twelve keys of Rhythm Changes. A reharmonization section is also provided which demonstrates how to reharmonize a chord progression on the spot.

Time Series

The Doing Time series presents a method for contacting, developing and relying on your internal time sense: This series is an excellent source for any musician who is serious about developing strong internal sense of time. This is particularly useful in any kind of music where the rhythms and time signatures may be very complex or free, and there is no conductor.

THE BIG METRONOME
Spiral Bound ISBN 1-890944-37-8   Perfect Bound ISBN 1890944-82-3

The Big Metronome is designed to help you develop a better internal sense of time. This is accomplished by requiring you to "feel time" rather than having you rely on the steady click of a metronome. The idea is to slowly wean yourself away from an external device and rely on your internal/natural sense of time. The exercises presented work in conjunction with the three CDs that accompany this book. CD 1 presents the first 13 settings from a traditional metronome 40-66; the second CD contains metronome markings 69-116, and the third CD contains metronome markings 120-208. The first CD gives you a 2 bar count off and a click every measure, the second CD gives you a 2 bar count off and a click every 2 measures, the 3rd CD gives you a 2 bar count off and a click every 4 measures. By presenting all common metronome markings a student can use these 3 CDs as a replacement for a traditional metronome.

Doing Time with the Blues Volume One:
Spiral Bound ISBN 1-890944-17-3   Perfect Bound ISBN 1890944-78-5

The book and CD presents a method for gaining an internal sense of time thereby eliminating dependence on a metronome. The book presents the basic concept for developing good time and also includes exercises that can be practiced with the CD. The CD provides eight 8 minute tracks at different tempos in which the time is delineated every 2 bars, and with an extra hit every 12 bars to outline the blues form. The student may then use the exercises presented in the book to gain control of their execution or improvise to gain control of their ideas using this bare minimum of time delineation.

Doing Time with the Blues Volume Two:
Spiral Bound ISBN 1-890944-18-1   Perfect Bound ISBN 1890944-79-3

This is the 2nd volume of a four volume series which presents a method for developing a musician's internal sense of time, thereby eliminating dependence on a metronome. This 2nd volume presents different exercises which further the development of this time sense. This 2nd volume begins to test even a professional level player's ability. The CD provides eight 8 minute tracks at different tempos in which the time is delineated every 4 bars with an extra hit every 12 bars to outline the blues form. New exercises are also included that can be practiced with the CD. This series is an excellent source for any musician who is serious about developing an internal sense of time.

Doing Time with 32 bars Volume One:
Spiral Bound ISBN 1-890944-22-X   Perfect Bound ISBN 1890944-80-7

The book and CD presents a method for gaining an internal sense of time thereby eliminating dependence on a metronome. The book presents the basic concept for developing good time and also includes exercises that can be practiced with the CD. The CD provides eight 8 minute tracks at different tempos in which the time is delineated every 2 bars, with an extra hit every 32 to outline the 32 bar form. The student may then use the exercises presented in the book to gain control of their execution or improvise to gain control of their ideas using this bare minimum of time delineation.

Doing Time with 32 bars Volume Two:
Spiral Bound ISBN 1-890944-23-8   Perfect Bound ISBN 1890944-81-5

This is the 2nd volume of a four volume series which presents a method for developing a musician's internal sense of time, thereby eliminating dependence on a metronome.. This 2nd volume presents different exercises which further the development of this time sense. This 2nd volume begins to test even a professional level player's ability. The CD provides eight 8 minute tracks at different tempos in which the time is delineated every 4 bars with an extra hit every 32 bars to outline the 32 bar form. New exercises are also included that can be practiced with the CD. This series is an excellent source for any musician who is serious about developing an internal sense of time.

Other Workbooks

Music Theory Workbook for All Instruments, Volume 1: Interval and Chord Construction
Spiral Bound ISBN 1890944-92-0   Perfect Bound ISBN 1890944-46-7

This book provides real hands-on application of intervals and chords. A theory section written in concise and easy to understand language prepares the student for all exercises. Worksheets are given that quiz a student about intervals and chord construction using staff notation. Answers are supplied in the back of the book enabling a student to work without a teacher.

E-Books

The Bruce Arnold series of instructional E-books is for the student who wishes to target specific areas of study that are of particular interest. Many of these books are excerpted from other larger texts. The excerpted source is listed for each book. These books are available on-line at www.muse-eek.com as well as at many e-tailers throughout the internet. These books can also be purchased in the traditional book binding format. (See the ISBN number for proper format)

Chord Velocity: Volume One, Learning to switch between chords quickly
E-book ISBN 1-890944-88-2   Traditional Book Binding ISBN 1-890944-97-1

The first hurdle a beginning guitarist encounters is difficulty in switching between chords quickly enough to make a chord progression sound like music. This book provides exercises that help a student gradually increase the speed with which they change chords. Special free audio files are also available on the muse-eek.com website to make practice more productive and fun. With a few weeks, remarkable improvement by can be achieved using this method. This book is excerpted from "1st Steps for a Beginning Guitarist Volume One."

Guitar Technique: Volume One, Learning the basics to fast, clean, accurate and fluid performance skills.
E-book ISBN 1-890944-91-2   Traditional Book Binding ISBN 1-890944-99-8

This book is for both the beginning guitarist or the more experienced guitarist who wishes to improve their technique. All aspects of the physical act of playing the guitar are covered, from how to hold a guitar to the specific way each hand is involved in the playing process. Pictures and videos are provided to help clarify each technique. These pictures and videos are either contained in the book or can be downloaded at www.muse-eek.com This book is excerpted from "1st Steps for a Beginning Guitarist Volume One."

Accompaniment: Volume One, Learning to Play Bass and Chords Simultaneously
E-book ISBN 1-890944-87-4   Traditional Book Binding ISBN 1-890944-96-3

The techniques found within this book are an excellent resource for creating and understanding how to play bass and chords simultaneously in a jazz or blues style. Special attention is paid to understanding how this technique is created, thereby enabling the student to recreate this style with other pieces of music. This book is excerpted from the book "Guitar Clinic."

Beginning Rhythm Studies: Volume One, Learning the basics of reading rhythm and playing in time.
E-book ISBN 1-890944-89-0   Traditional Book Binding 1-890944-98-X

This book covers the basics for anyone wishing to understand or improve their rhythmic abilities. Simple language is used to show the student how to read and play rhythm. Exercises are presented which can accelerate the learning process. Audio examples in the form of midifiles are available on the muse-eek.com website to facilitate learning the correct rhythm in time. This book is excerpted from the book "Rhythm Primer."